MW01102611

The New Gl⊕bal Society

Globalization, Language, and Culture

The New Global Society

The New Global Society

Globalization, Language, and Culture

Richard Lee
State University of New York
College at Oneonta

Foreword by
James Bacchus
Chairman, Global Trade Practice Group
of Greenberg Traurig, Professional Association

Introduction by
Ilan Alon, Ph.D.
Crummer Graduate School of Business
Rollins College

CHELSEA HOUSE
P U B L I S H E R S
A Haights Cross Communications Company ®
Philadelphia

COVER: Three Hindu women walk down a street in Little India, Singapore.

CHELSEA HOUSE PUBLISHERS

VP, NEW PRODUCT DEVELOPMENT Sally Cheney
DIRECTOR OF PRODUCTION Kim Shinners
CREATIVE MANAGER Takeshi Takahashi
MANUFACTURING MANAGER Diann Grasse

Staff for GLOBALIZATION, LANGUAGE, AND CULTURE

EXECUTIVE EDITOR Lee Marcott
EDITORIAL ASSISTANT Carla Greenberg
PRODUCTION EDITOR Noelle Nardone
PHOTO EDITOR Sarah Bloom
SERIES AND COVER DESIGNER Keith Trego
LAYOUT 21st Century Publishing and Communications, Inc.

A Haights Cross Communications ✈ Company ®

www.chelseahouse.com

First Printing

9 8 7 6 5 4 3 2 1

Library of Congress Cataloging-in-Publication Data

Lee, Richard, 1957–
    Globalization, language, and culture/Richard Lee.
        p. cm.—(The new global society)
    Includes bibliographical references and index.
    ISBN 0-7910-8189-3 (hard cover)
 1. Culture and globalization. 2. Language and culture. I. Title. II. Series.
HM621.L44 2005
303.48'2'09—dc22

                                    2005009589

Contents

For Michael

Foreword

by James Bacchus

IT'S A SMALL WORLD AFTER ALL

One reason that I know this is true is because I have a daughter who adores Walt Disney World in my hometown of Orlando, Florida. When Jamey was small, she and I would go to Walt Disney World together. We would stand together in a long line waiting to ride her very favorite ride—"Small World." We would stand together in those long lines over and over again.

Jamey is in high school now, but, of course, she still adores Walt Disney World, and she and I still stand together from time to time in those same long lines—because she never tires of seeing "Small World." She is not alone. Seemingly endless lines of children have stood waiting for that same ride through the years, hand in hand with their parents, waiting for the chance to take the winding boat ride through Disney's "Small World." When their chance has come, they have seen the vast variety of the world in which we live unfold along the winding way as it appears to the child in all of us. Hundreds of dancing dolls adorn an array of diverse and exotic settings from around the world. In the echoing voice of a song they sing together— over and over again—they remind all those along for the ride that ours is a world of laughter, a world of tears, a world of hopes, and a world of fears.

And so it is. So it appears when we are children, and so it surely appears when we put childhood behind us and try to assume our new roles as "grown-ups" in what is supposed to be the adult world. The laughter, the tears, the hopes, the fears, are all still there in a world that, to our grown-up eyes, keeps getting smaller every day. And, even when we are no longer children, even when we are now grown-ups, we don't really know what to do about it.

The grown-up name for our small world is "globalization." Our globalizing world is getting smaller every day. Economically and otherwise, our world is becoming a place where we all seem to be taking the same ride. Advances in information, transportation, and many other technologies are making distance disappear, and are making next-door neighbors of all of us, whatever our nationality, whatever our costume, whatever the song we sing.

When Walt Disney first introduced the "Small World" ride at the World's Fair in New York in 1964, I was in high school, and we could still pretend that, although the world was getting smaller, it still consisted of many different places. But no more. The other day, I took a handheld device, called a "BlackBerry," out of my pocket and e-mailed instructions to a colleague in my law firm regarding a pending legal matter. I was on a train in the Bavarian mountains in Germany, while my colleague was thousands of miles away in the United States. In effect, we were in the same small place.

This is just one example of our ever-smaller world. And, however small it seems to me in my middle age, and however smaller it may become in my lifetime, it is likely to shrink all the more for my daughter Jamey and for every other young American attending high school today.

Hence, we announce this new series of books for high school students on some of the results of globalization. These results inspire hope, shown in the efforts of so many around the world to respond to the challenges posed by

globalization by making international laws, building international institutions, and seeking new ways to live and work
together in our smaller world. Those results also inspire
fear, as evidenced by streets filled with anti-globalization
protesters in Seattle, London, and other globalized cities
around the world.

It is hard to tell truth from fiction in assessing the results of
globalization. The six volumes in this series help us to do so.
Does globalization promote worldwide economic development, or does it hinder it? Does it reduce poverty, or does it
increase it? Does it enhance culture, or does it harm it? Does
it advance the cause of human rights, or does it impede it?
Does it serve the cause of workers' rights, or does it slow it?
Does it help the environment, or does it hurt it? These are the
important questions posed in these volumes. The hope is that
in asking these questions the series will help young people
find answers to them that will prove to be better than those
found thus far by "grown-ups."

I have had the privilege of trying to begin the process of
finding some of these answers. I have helped negotiate international trade agreements for the United States. I have served
as a member of the Congress of the United States. I have been
one of seven jurists worldwide on the court of final appeal
that helps the 148 countries that are Members of the World
Trade Organization to uphold international trade rules and
to peacefully resolve international trade disputes. I am one of
these who see far more reason for hope than for fear in the
process of globalization.

I believe we will all be more likely to see globalization in this
way if we recall the faces of the dancing dolls in Disney's
"Small World." Those dolls are from many different countries.
They wear many different costumes. But their faces are very
much the same. The song they sing is the same. And, in that
song, they remind us all that as we all ride together, "There's so

much that we share, that it's time we're aware it's a small world, after all." Indeed it is. And, if we remember all that we in the world share—if we remember above all, our shared humanity—then we will be much more likely to make globalization a reason to hope that our smaller world will also be a better world.

James Bacchus
Chairman, Global Trade Practice Group
of Greenberg Traurig, Professional Association
April 2005

Introduction

by Ilan Alon

Globalization is now an omnipresent phenomenon in society, economics, and politics, affecting industry and government, and all other walks of life in one form or another. THE NEW GLOBAL SOCIETY series gives the reader a well-rounded understanding of the forces of globalization and its multifaceted impact on our world. The international flavor is evident in the make-up of the authors in the series, who include one Israeli, one New Zealander, one Bulgarian, one Korean, and two American scholars. In addition to an international slate of authors, many of whom have lived and worked around the world, the writers hail from fields as diverse as economics, business, comparative literature, and journalism. Their varied experiences and points of view bring a comprehensive and diverse analysis to the topics they write about.

While the books were written to stand alone, those readers who complete all six will find many points of commonality between the books and many instances where observations from one book can be directly applied to points made in another.

These books are written for the lay person and include definitions of key terms and ideas and many examples that help the reader make the ideas more concrete. The books are short and non-technical and are intended to spur the reader to read more about globalization outside these books and in other sources such as magazines, newspapers, journals, Internet sources, and other books on the topics. The discussion of the positive and negative aspects of the consequences of globalization, both here and abroad, will allow the reader to make their own judgments about the merits and demerits of globalization.

A brief description of each of the six books in the series follows:

Globalization and Development—Eugene D. Jaffe
Eugene D. Jaffe of the Graduate School of Business, Bar-Ilan University, Israel, and current Visiting Professor at Copenhagen Business School, Denmark, explains the key terms and concepts of globalization and its historical development. Specifically, it ties globalization to economic development and examines globalization's impact on both developed and developing countries. Arguments for and against globalization are presented. The relevance of globalization for the American economy is specifically addressed.

There are many illustrations of the concepts through stories and case examples, photographs, tables, and diagrams. After reading this book, students should have a good understanding of the positive and negative aspects of globalization and will be better able to understand the issues as they appear in the press and other media.

Globalization and Labor—Peter Enderwick
Peter Enderwick is Professor of International Business, Auckland University of Technology, New Zealand, and a long-time researcher on international labor issues. His book provides a discussion of the impact of globalization on labor with a focus on employment, earnings, staffing strategies, and human resource management within global business. Contemporary issues and concerns such as offshore sourcing, labor standards, decreasing social mobility, and income inequality are treated. The book contains many case examples and vignettes illustrating that while globalization creates

both winners and losers, there are opportunities to increase the beneficial effects through appropriate policy.

Globalization and Poverty—Nadejda Ballard

Nadejda Ballard is a professional international business consultant with clients in the United States and Europe and is an adjunct instructor for international business at Rollins College, Winter Park, Florida. In addition to her extensive experience living and working in various countries, Nadejda is also a native of Bulgaria, a developing country that is struggling with many of the issues discussed in her book.

Globalization, which is reshaping our society at all levels from the individual to the national and regional, is also changing the way we define poverty and attempt to combat it. The book includes the ideas of academics and researchers as well as those who are charged at the practical level with grappling with the issues of world poverty. Unlike other books on the subject, her aim is not to promote a certain view or theory, but to provide a realistic overview of the current situation and the strategies intended to improve it. The book is rich with such visual aids as maps, photographs, tables, and charts.

Globalization and the Environment—Ho-Won Jeong

Howon Jeong teaches at the Institute for Conflict Analysis and Resolution at George Mason University and is author of *Global Environmental Policymaking*. His new book for Chelsea House discusses the major global impacts of human activities on the environment including global warming, ozone depletion, the loss of biological diversity, deforestation, and soil erosion, among other topics. This book explores the interrelationship of human life and nature. The earth has finite resources and our every action has consequences for the future. The effects of human consumption and pollution are felt in every corner of the globe. How we choose to live will affect generations to come. The book should generate an awareness of the ongoing degradation of our environment and it is hoped that this awareness will serve as a catalyst for action needed to be undertaken for and by future generations.

Globalization, Culture, and Language—Richard E. Lee
Richard E. Lee teaches world literature and critical theory at the College of Oneonta, State University of New York. The author believes that globalization is a complex phenomenon of contemporary life, but one with deep ties to the past movements of people and ideas around the world. By placing globalization within this historical context, the author casts the reader as part of those long-term cultural trends.

The author recognizes that his American audience is largely composed of people who speak one language. He introduces such readers to the issues related to a multilingual, global phenomenon. Readers will also learn from the book that the cultural impacts of globalization are not merely a one-way street from the United States to the rest of the world. The interconnectedness of the modern world means that the movements of ideas and people affect everyone.

Globalization and Human Rights—Alma Kadragic
Alma Kadragic is a journalist, a writer, and an adjunct professor at Phoenix University. She was a writer and producer for ABC News in New York, Washington D.C., and London for 16 years. From 1983–89 she was ABC News bureau chief in Warsaw, Poland, and led news coverage of the events that led to the fall of Communism in Poland, Hungary, Czechoslovakia, East Germany, and Yugoslavia.

Her book links two of the fundamental issues of our time: globalization and human rights. Human rights are the foundation on which the United States was established in the late

18th century. Today, guarantees of basic human rights are included in the constitutions of most countries.

The author examines the challenges and opportunities globalization presents for the development of human rights in many countries. Globalization often brings changes to the way people live. Sometimes these changes expand human rights, but sometimes they threaten them. Both the positive and negative impacts of globalization on personal freedom and other measures of human rights are examined. She also considers how the globalization of the mass media can work to protect the human rights of individuals in any country.

All of the books in THE NEW GLOBAL SOCIETY series examine both the pros and the cons of the consequences of globalization in an objective manner. Taken together they provide the readers with a concise and readable introduction to one of the most pervasive and fascinating phenomena of our time.

Dr. Ilan Alon, Ph.D
Crummer Graduate School of Business
Rollins College
April 2005

The Treaty of Tordesillas in 1494

On the morning of September 5, 1494, a despondent King John II of Portugal sat at a table with his advisors. They were in Lisbon debating a treaty that had already been ratified on July 2 by the rulers of Spain, King Ferdinand and Queen Isabella. King John pondered the sequence of events that had led him to this table, where he would ratify the Treaty of Tordesillas. Portugal's navigators had helped to expand Portugal's trade routes. Remarkable feats such as one by explorer Bartholomew Dias had made Portugal the envy of other seafaring nations. Dias had returned to Lisbon in 1488 from a two-year voyage that eventually led him well below the equator. Dias sailed so far south along the western coast of Africa that the North Star—

the point all European sailors needed to orient by—
vanished below the horizon! A vicious storm pushed Dias's
ship far out of sight of land and far to the south. When the
storm allowed, he found that land could be sighted to his
north. He had sailed around the tip of Africa.

The commitment to exploration and the seafaring skills
of Portuguese navigators such as Dias had enabled King
John to feel that he had bested the Spanish politically as
well as militarily. After all, it had been only fifteen years
earlier, in 1479, that a peace treaty between Spain and
Portugal had ended four years of fierce fighting. Although
Portugal was often defeated in land battles in Europe itself,
Portuguese ships consistently beat Spanish ships in naval
encounters. Only in the Canary Islands, off the western coast
of Africa, had Spain prevailed. In fact, a papal decision,
called a Papal Bull—the most respected legal statement
one could hope for in 15th-century Europe—was issued
in 1481 that concerned the Spanish and Portuguese.
Although kings and queens maintained secular control
over their domains, papal authority—the approval of the
Catholic Church—cut across and codified many secular
decisions. This Bull had decreed that all lands discovered
south of the Canary Islands would belong to Portugal.
King John had been confident that the new areas that
would be discovered would help him to further establish
Portugal as a great kingdom. Even though he faced great
competition from Spain, all other European rulers had
been excluded from potential control of newly discovered
lands in the golden lands to the west and south. According
to another papal bull issued in 1493, which continued the
logic of the 1481 decree, only Spain and Portugal would be
able to lay claim to newly discovered lands in the "New
World." However, Ferdinand and Isabella had been able to
influence the Spanish-born Pope Alexander VI. He decreed

in the 1493 decision that all lands to the west of an imaginary line about 300 miles from the Canary Islands would belong to Spain. Immediately after the Pope's decree, King John II began negotiations with the Spanish rulers, and the result was the Treaty of Tordesillas, signed in Tordesillas, Spain, on June 7, 1494.

The Portuguese King was taking a calculated risk by ratifying this treaty. It did extend the line of Spanish control further to the west than the previous decree had allowed. However, no one knew how much land there was to the west of the new line of demarcation—the imaginary line that divided Spanish from Portuguese areas of control. King John had been able to get his negotiators to insist upon one important point in Tordesillas: the line of demarcation should extend all the way around the world. After all, now that all educated people agreed that the world was round, not flat, such a line of demarcation should extend around the sphere. New maps would need to be made, maps that would ultimately limit Spain's ability to control the rich, as yet uncharted lands of Asia. King John decided he would sign the treaty, hoping that the lands still to be discovered to the east of the line, which was now about 1,100 miles to the west of the Cape Verde Islands (further to the south and west than the Canary Islands), would be profitable and substantial.

THE PARADOX OF A TREATY THAT DIVIDES THE WORLD IN TWO
The Treaty of Tordesillas divided the world in half—one part for Spain, one for Portugal—but this division is actually a very important event in the history of globalization. Although there are many ways to define this key term, **globalization** can generally be taken to mean the trend toward a single, integrated, and interdependent world. As we shall see, this simple definition is not entirely accurate, but it is an important beginning. But how can a treaty that divides the world be a step in the direction of unification?

On June 7, 1494, the first major international consequence of Christopher Columbus's famous 1492 expedition to the New World occurred. That day marked the official signing of the Treaty of Tordesillas (It would later be ratified separately by Spain and Portugal). While Columbus's return to Spain after he landed in what is now Hispaniola (which is itself now divided into the countries of Haiti and the Dominican Republic) was noteworthy for many reasons—including the introduction into Europe of items such as tobacco—it was the geopolitical consequence of his return that is especially important to students of globalization. At the Treaty of Tordesillas, the official language of diplomacy, statecraft (and thus of trade)—Latin—was used to signify the importance of the treaty. Latin was the language used in important matters by all educated people in Europe up until about 1700. Every nation–state needed to conduct its official, interstate business in what would come to be called a **lingua franca**, a common language and a language of political power. Latin's role as the official language was due to the power and control exercised over the European monarchic families by the Holy Roman Empire, whose central institution was the Catholic Church.

The intersection of the power and influence of language upon culture—and ultimately upon social, economic, and political spheres—is the subject of this book. The intersection of language, maps, and the history of globalization is the web that must first be spun so that the larger intersections can be viewed. Throughout this text, we will focus on how culture and language operate and on the consequences of these interactions. The text will locate some moments of historical interest as a context within which to view elements central to the relationship between globalization and culture. Ultimately, the immense complexity and variability of the relationship between globalization and culture is not served by simplistic definitions. This text will deepen your understanding of the issue for your future research interests, even as it introduces a key component of globalization: the impact on and influence of elements of culture and language.

The Treaty of Tordesillas divided the world into two, yet it was a key step in the direction of global unity because the division was accomplished by an institution that was perceived to be in control of the whole world. The control of the Pope in making the decision—made authoritative by codifying the treaty in the official language, Latin, to which all other languages must defer—was also an illusion. Other European countries such as Britain and France eventually ignored the idea that only Spain and Portugal had spheres of influence in the New World and colonized when they were able. Further, the native populations of the lands that had been "divided" were certainly not aware of the pretense of universal control wielded by the Papal Bull (or by Spanish and Portuguese rulers, for that matter). These **indigenous** or native people would, however, be very much affected by this early extension of economic power and cultural influence. In this way, we can see that although the concept of a movement toward a unified system may be ignored by or involve individuals unaware of that movement, it nonetheless has an undeniable effect on even those parties who try to ignore or remain unaware.

Additionally, the paradox of a treaty that divides being a marker for unification helps further the focus of this book because it illustrates a central issue related to language: namely, that language use can always be viewed as a tension between the tendency of language to move toward one, "official" version and the opposing tendency of a given language's spread into multiple dialects. We can call this a "push-me/pull-you" tendency (a centralizing force offset by a decentralizing force), and it is a concept central to the development of an understanding of how languages, maps, and culture are interrelated—and key to an understanding of how globalization works in our world.

Ultimately, however, even a sense that there is one concept (such as globalization) that is opposed by some other concept (local, cultural forces) is a vast oversimplification of a very complicated dynamic. By this we mean that there are many competing forces in flux, rather than any single force acting upon others. As a way of focusing in on this complex of forces, however, the initial understanding of the forces themselves—operating in what we have called a "push–pull" circuit—is a beginning. An essential understanding of the relationships among globalization's cultural components relies upon what we can call an "Americanization of the world." As an example of the complicated and fragmented nature of the globalization–culture relationship, anthropologist Arjun Appuradai, in his article entitled "Disjuncture and Difference in the Global Cultural Economy," writes that

> it is worth noticing that for the people of Irian Jaya, Indonesia-nization may be more worrisome than Americanization, as Japanization may be for Koreans, Indianization for Sri Lankans, Vietnamization for the Cambodians, Russianization for the people of Soviet Armenia and the Baltic Republics . . . . For polities of smaller scale, there is always a fear of cultural absorption by polities of larger scale, especially those that are near by.[1]

The Treaty of Tordesillas is a useful example for beginning to understand the idea of globalization and recognizing that an oversimplified beginning will need further complication at some later time. When the Pope assumed that he could divide the world, he assumed a cultural power that he did not have; however, there were very real consequences to the act of division. In the same manner, thinking about globalization as only a two-way (push–pull) operation, a tension between the forces of the West and the rest of the almost innumerable cultural groups in the world, puts us in the position of the Spanish: bound by the forces in operation and forced to think about the Treaty as if its tenets were in fact always enforceable. The Spanish and Portuguese monarchs, however, were subject to more subtle, if equally powerful, forces, whether they were aware of them or not.

We urge the reader of this text to be an active reader, synthesizing the various concepts that will be presented. This attempt will be rewarded in that a good beginning will have been made toward understanding one of the most complex events in your world. You are part of world culture, and it is in your best interests to be aware of and understand it.

We will refer back to the Treaty of Tordesillas later in this text. The organizational structure of the book is planned around a focus that will move you from a general understanding of the concepts related to globalization's cultural effects to specific instances that will help illustrate the particulars at the heart of this general phenomenon. In Chapter 2, "Globalization and Culture: Two Views," we will explore the extreme ends of the spectrum of opinion on globalization's impact on culture. Chapter 3, "Culture and Ideology," will clarify the core components—the abstractions—necessary for getting beyond one-sided opinions on this multifaceted issue. Chapter 4, "The Pre-History of Globalization," will make the case that our moment in historical time is not the first in which cultural beliefs in one dominant culture have affected people at a far remove from the source of the dominant culture's control.

In Chapter 5, "Maps and Language," we link language to culture, introducing the visual analogy of "mapping"—cartography—as a way of understanding the crucial role that language-use plays in cultural formation. Further, a brief introduction to competing theories of linguistics (specifically concerned with language acquisition and how one forms ideas about one's culture) will lead to a firmer understanding of what is called **ideology**: the often invisible assumptions that support social activities. In all cases, the intent throughout the book is to introduce complicated concepts using concrete examples, while still allowing for further study. Chapter 6, "Language, Culture, and Politics," summarizes and extends many of the comments discussed to that point, setting the stage for Chapters 7, "The Transmission of the Modernist Dream: Ideological and Cultural Transfers," and Chapter 8, "The Movement of Goods and People." Chapter 9 provides a brief conclusion. Examples of the nuances of financial, cultural, and demographic (people-based) interactions are developed here, so that you can begin to analyze the productions of culture with which you are familiar—such as movies, music, and literature. Each chapter will build upon that which has gone before, but students may well benefit by re-reading some chapters, since later chapters will often refer back to ideas presented earlier in the book.

Globalization and Culture: Two Views

These three commentators summarize the range of opinions on the worldwide interconnection of economic and cultural systems that is called globalization. Social commentator Thomas Friedman—who has written several books about globalization and whose political column appears regularly in the *New York Times*—observes that the tendency of businesses to seek out the most cost-effective ways to produce their goods and service their customers is a normal outgrowth of rational business methods. This worldwide movement of capital investment— money moving at lightning speed to seek out better rates of return— has had overwhelmingly positive economic and social benefits for the populations of less-developed countries, according to Friedman. He notes that the communications revolution (television, microprocessors for computers, and cellular technologies, among others) has enabled businesses to seek out the lowest prices for production and distribution of their goods and services.

Joseph Stiglitz, a winner of the Nobel Prize for Economics, argues that the economic policies of developed countries and international businesses—often poorly suited to the on-the-ground realities of developing countries—actually do more harm than good. Stiglitz observes that many opponents of global interconnectedness worry that global monetary policies often take place regardless of the needs of *all* the people on the globe.

David Morris, vice president of the Institute for Local Self-Reliance (an organization that generally takes a dim view of "planetary corporate rule"), is one of a number of critics of globalization who argue against what they see as the soulless spread of an economic system that has dire cultural and social effects on the cultures of countries used as economic staging points. They decry the homogenization—the sameness—of a shallow international (often American) cultural standard, even as they argue that the increases in standards of living for developing countries are not as dramatic as globalization's supporters claim. At the heart of arguments such as those put forth by Morris is a business truism: a corporation owes no loyalty to anything other than profits for its shareholders. Although there are certainly companies that we associate with countries—IBM with America, or Qantas airlines with Australia, for example—the realities of today's global marketplace (according to Morris's version of the argument) punish companies who adhere to national loyalties when the movement of jobs and investments to overseas venues will yield higher profits.

Friedman is a proponent of the reality of globalization: he believes that noble cultural and social effects flow from the interconnectedness that is the heart of globalization. Increased concern for human rights, the establishment of democratic governments that allow all people to have a say in their governments, and even freedom from the fear of war, all of these—and much more—have been claimed as benefits of globalization. At the other extreme, opponents of the global movement of culture and capital argue that the most powerful players in the global marketplace act without a mandate aside from profit. Further, say such critics, popular culture's international reach has meant the death of individual cultural integrity. Local cultures in places around the world will be lost in favor of a sort of "global" culture that treats exotic cultures as trends to be enjoyed briefly, while all the while the dominance of Western popular culture buries the authenticity and uniqueness of these cultures. There is a broad middle ground between these two extremes, between Friedman and Morris—one that theorists like Stiglitz explore—but it is worth mentioning the two ends of the argument in order to understand the debate itself.

THE INEVITABILITY ARGUMENT IN FAVOR OF GLOBALIZATION

There is no way to un-know a technology. Although the world might well be better off if certain technologies had never been invented—including nuclear fission, the ability to synthesize dangerous chemicals, and others—invention and discovery are a reality. Perhaps the absence of nuclear weapons during the Cold War period from 1945 until 1990 would have made the terrifying standoff between the United States and the then-U.S.S.R. less potentially devastating. Perhaps the absence of chemical weapons and nerve gas would make the idea of war less of a horror in general. The embrace of change and innovation, however, is part of Western culture.

The case of The Treaty of Tordesillas is instructive: the technological advantages in navigation, metal-crafting, and warfare that the Spanish and Portuguese explorers held over the indigenous cultures they encountered guaranteed that whatever political and social demands these Europeans desired would hold sway. According to some, while it is disturbing to consider the calamitous effects of European and native contact—genocide, for example—the technological superiority of Europeans made the destruction of native cultures a possibility. The elimination of native cultures ultimately resulted in the growth of free states and other vibrant cultures. While there is a certain callousness to the argument by inevitability, the scenario is reminiscent of a term that appears often in the literature of globalization: "creative destruction." This refers to the demonstrable fact that the emergence of a new **paradigm**—a word that refers to the overall set of assumptions behind the way the world works—involves the destabilization of the old order. The old gives way to the new, often to the detriment of those invested in the old order.

Other forms of technological innovation power the current globalizing trend. What is generally referred to as globalization—the movement toward a single, interdependent, and integrated world—has been powered by a revolution in communications technology. The development of the microchip—the brain of every computer—has made it possible to communicate with most parts of the world almost instantaneously. Compare the seconds a cell phone call to Europe takes to the weeks it took Columbus to land in what is now the Dominican Republic in 1492. Information processing—and the ability to act upon the information—is how businesses operate efficiently. And efficiency—rationalization—is also at the core of Western culture.

The Cost of Baseballs

As an example of how access to information can help you to dominate a market, imagine yourself a baseball player for a local team that has a very limited budget. You need baseballs to play together, but you play most of your games near a large river, and players routinely hit balls into it. Another teammate has been selling the team baseballs he has purchased at the only store in town for the cost of the balls plus a small markup for his trouble; he charges $4.00 per ball. You receive a phone call from a cousin in Cooperstown, New York, who mentions that his town is baseball-crazy: he sells baseballs at $1.00 per ball. You do have to figure out a way to get the balls from your cousin to you, but, assuming that shipping charges are reasonable (or a timely visit is planned), you can either save your team a lot of money or make a large profit by selling your balls to the team at $3.00 per ball. Four things are involved in this simple example: access to local information (the price of balls in your town and Cooperstown), the needs of a given market (your team's inability to keep the balls out of the river, combined with the fact that your town has only one store selling baseballs), additional costs of doing business beyond production costs (in this case, any delivery charges), and access to the market (without awareness of the team's current situation, neither the team nor your own pocket would benefit).

This example of the baseballs may seem silly, but it is the central reality of the economic engine that is globalization. The four elements in our example show us how globalization operates in financial markets: instantaneous access to information on local costs, instantaneous knowledge of a market's needs, instantaneous (and almost free) data transfer using the Internet, and a willingness to trade on consumer needs in developing countries that are influenced by the global reach of American and European popular culture. This last component is particularly important: the development of a stable class of consumers is connected to rising standards of living throughout the world and to the rise of democratic institutions, as consumers increasingly want the things they see. In other words, everyone wants a cheaper baseball.

Thomas Friedman writes that "globalization has replaced the Cold War as the defining international system."[5] He and many others see the stark division of the world into two spheres—an American and a Soviet—as having given way to a different structure: one based upon "integration":

> The world has become an increasingly interwoven place, and today, whether you are a company or a country, your threats and opportunities increasingly derive from who you are connected to. This globalization system is also characterized by a single word: the *Web*. So, in the broadest sense we have gone from a system built around division and walls to a system increasingly built around integration and webs.[6]

Proponents of globalization believe in a version of the cliché that a rising tide lifts all boats. The elimination of trade barriers—traditionally used by countries to protect their national industries—will allow the marketplace to adjust itself. With free trade—the watchword of internationalists who espouse global economic interconnectedness—will come free countries and freed peoples. Authoritarian governments will be forced to yield to the need for humanitarian reforms if they wish to participate in the global economy. Trade compacts between nations such as the North American Free Trade Agreement (NAFTA)—which dramatically reduced trade restrictions among most of the countries in North and Central America—lower the barriers to free trade that countries have traditionally erected to allow their companies to hold onto their national markets.

THE NIGHTMARE SCENARIO OF
THE ANTIGLOBALIZATION "MOVEMENT"

The greatest fear of those opposed to globalizing tendencies is that economic policies will increasingly be made by individuals and institutions elected by no one, that there is no accountability besides the profit motive and no loyalty or connections to established, sovereign national entities. The scenario presented in Chapter 1 on the Treaty of Tordesillas provides a version of these critics' greatest concern. That treaty—which divided the resources of the newly discovered, resource-rich worlds of North, Central, and South America—was made by an extragovernmental agency (the Catholic Church, led by the Pope) with no concern or thought for the already vibrant cultures that existed in the "new world." A decision made for the good of Spain and Portugal excluded all other European countries, and allowed for the economic development of these two countries to the exclusion of all others. The notion that the "light" of Catholic belief would be spread to ignorant pagans in the new world—a central ideology behind the subjugation of native peoples around the world during the colonizing activities of countries in the 16th through the 19th centuries—is equivalent to the belief that democracy and Western-style human rights will follow in the wake of economic interdependence. This connection—between cultural "enlightenment" and economic activity—is a key argument used by supporters of globalization.

Additionally, globalization is not something that one "supports." In other words, no one group is able to vote against or influence the tendency of markets to seek profitability. Two authors opposed to a simplistic embrace of globalization, Sarah Anderson and John Cavanaugh, write that "The World Bank argues that accelerated globalization has coincided with greater world equality. . . . However, during the period of rapid globalization of the 1980s and 1990s, the gap between rich and poor within most nations has widened."[7] For opponents of the rushing tide of free trade and free markets, the reality of a high-minded belief that the rising waters of globalization will create opportunities for better lives in developing countries (often called the Third World) has been a misleading one. For protestors at economic summit meetings involving the world's major developed countries, wage inequality is an indicator of the generally disastrous effects of open trade policies and economic interdependence (Figure 2.1). **Wage inequality** is a measure of the relative distributions of incomes; this measure tracks the disparity within countries of high- and low-wage earners. But

Figure 2.1 Thousands of antiglobalization militants demonstrate in Paris on November 15, 2003 to mark the end of the second European Social Forum, an international gathering of antiglobalization and antiwar groups. For these opponents of globalization, the promise of better opportunities for people around the world has not been realized. Their frustration has fueled militant protests around the world in the 1980s, 1990s, and into the 21st century.

even large-scale protests at meetings of the world's economic heavyweights, the so-called G8 countries—Canada, France, Germany, Italy, Japan, Russia, the United Kingdom, and the United States—have had little appreciable effect on globalization's tidal movement.

According to United Nations and World Bank statistics, over 30 former Communist and other developing economies report greater wage inequality since trade reforms have allowed greater foreign investment. The loosening of national controls over trade restrictions and tariffs (fees imposed on imports) is generally referred to as **economic liberalization**. Countries that have seen a widening gap between the wealthiest and the poorest in their countries include Argentina, Bulgaria, Chile, China, the Dominican Republic, Ecuador, Estonia, Ethiopia, Ghana, Hungary, Kazakhstan, Mexico, Nigeria, Poland, Romania, Russia, Taiwan, Ukraine, and Uruguay.[8] More surprising, perhaps, is the fact that inequality is sharply higher in many industrialized countries as well. Common sense would lead one to suppose that the citizens in developed countries would generally benefit from policies that create greater economic freedom. However, according to some researchers, wage inequality has increased in the following countries as well: Australia, Germany, Japan, Sweden, the United States, and the United Kingdom.[9]

Opponents of extragovernmental control of national economies reject the argument that increasing liberalization of trade policies creates a rising tide that lifts all boats. The "nightmare scenario" of the antiglobalization movement is that corporations will flit from profitable locale to profitable locale, always searching for the easiest way to cut costs, regardless of the impact on the citizens of the nations involved. The rush to a de facto one-world government elected by no one will lead to a homogenized global culture that replicates the forms of American (Western) culture. Discussing the fate of local cultures when faced with the juggernaut of global popular culture, Tyler Cowen, a professor of economics at George Mason University, writes,

> The argument that markets destroy culture and diversity comes from people across the political spectrum. Liberal political scientist Benjamin Barber claims that the world is poised between *jihad*, a "bloody politics of identity," and McWorld, "a bloodless economics of profit," represented by the spread of McDonald's and American popular culture. In *False Dawn: The Delusions of Global Capitalism* (1998), the English conservative John Gray denounces globalization as a dangerous delusion, a product of the hopelessly utopian Enlightenment dream of a "single, world-wide civilization in which the varied traditions and cultures of the past were superseded by a new, universal community founded in reason."[10]

Figure 2.2 In this picture, the ancient pagodas of the Forbidden City are surrounded by the modern buildings of Beijing, but in other cities, such as Shanghai, the rush to modernize has led to the destruction of many buildings of great beauty and historical value.

A possibly greater threat contained within the economic interdependence that is globalization involves cultural and social oppression by industrialized nations over local cultures. Since English is the language of international trade, and since English is the language of 80 percent of the data in the world's computers,[11] there is an inherent threat of linguistic imperialism imposed on non-English-speaking cultures. Imperialism refers to the process by which colonies are controlled and dominated. Linguistic imperialism denotes the "colonizing" tendencies of languages— such as English, the primary language of international business and of American popular culture. In order to establish a foundation for understanding this imposition—and the overall effect of globalization's worldwide cultural impact—a survey of how language operates and of prior waves of globalization (especially insofar as language is concerned) are both necessary.

CRITICAL THINKING AND LOGICAL FALLACIES

This chapter introduced the two extremes of belief that make up general thinking on globalization. A word about **logical fallacies**—mistakes in thinking—is in order. Although people like to think that their beliefs and opinions are firmly grounded in fact and logic, this is unfortunately not always the case. Very often, people substitute logical fallacies for logic. This chapter will briefly mention some qualifications that readers should keep in mind while analyzing the remainder of this book. Essentially, all readers should practice critical thinking, or careful thinking, when presented with new information, and a survey of just what is meant by logical fallacies in particular and critical thinking in general is a good way to do this. One example of a logical fallacy will suffice for now.

A false dichotomy—sometimes called a false dilemma—is one type of logical fallacy. A false dichotomy presents only two choices in a given situation. A reasoned analysis of the situation, however, usually reveals that there are other options than the two presented. In the scenario presented in this chapter, we said that there is a wide gray area between the two extremes presented. Globalization is a very sophisticated and complex topic that involves the interrelationships between and among such diverse fields as economics, linguistics, politics, and socio-cultural activities. As a result, it is easy to get lost in all the detail. By presenting the two extremes of thinking on the issue of globalization (one for, one against) it is possible to set up a general set of statements that will introduce students to this complex issue. The danger, however, is that readers will believe that globalization is an either–or phenomenon. In other words, one is either firmly in favor of globalization or one is firmly against it. This is an example of a false dichotomy, because there is a wide spectrum of possible opinions between the two extremes. Perhaps a clearer example of a false dichotomy is when students are told, "Do well in school or you will not succeed in life." While there is little doubt that good study skills, attention to detail, and the ability to plan and construct projects—the kinds of things that will get you good grades—are also skills that will help you succeed in your life, there is not necessarily any relationship between getting "A's" in school and your ultimate success as a human being. The world is full of people who were poor students but are successful and who are content with their lives. This does not necessarily mean that success in life comes from failing at school, however. Critical thinking means that you avoid jumping to conclusions in favor of evaluating the logical connections and implications of statements.

Your job as a reader is to be a critical thinker. This means that you need to sift through the information presented, using whatever explanations and analogies this book presents as a map for your introductory understanding. The glossary at the end of the book and the suggested readings will help you to be a better consumer of information on complex concepts like globalization.

Culture and Ideology

A WORKING DEFINITION OF THE WORD "CULTURE"

Although it should be clear by now that globalization is a term that implies a weaving together of such topics as economics, politics, and culture, the primary focus of this text is on the ways in which culture and globalization are related—a focus that implies anthropological and sociological components. The term **culture**, which will be used here to refer to all the ways in which people live in their daily lives, is a particularly tricky and general term, one that requires some attention. A particularly apt definition, by respected author John Tomlinson, puts it as follows: "Culture for my purposes refers to all these mundane practices that directly contribute to people's ongoing 'life-narratives': the stories by which we, chronically, interpret our existence."[12] Tomlinson's use of the word "mundane" does not suggest "boring."

Rather he is emphasizing the fact that culture is an all day, everyday phenomenon, one that pervades daily life. This chapter will introduce the idea that the ways in which individuals around the globe live their everyday lives is increasingly a function of cultural trends that are not always rooted in the places where they live. Further, a distinction will need to be made between culture—which means "actions"—and **ideology**—the set of assumptions that condition why one acts as one does. Although the terms are sometimes used interchangeably (culture used as shorthand for beliefs and action), it is useful to differentiate between belief systems and the actions that flow from those beliefs.

Tomlinson underlines a key aspect of culture when he explains that human beings make sense of the world around them based upon a large set of often-invisible assumptions that structure their daily lives. In America, and in much of Western civilization in general, these assumptions include such things as a sense that individual aspirations matter (and that individuals are responsible for achieving their goals); that one should look, act, and speak in certain ways that are consistent with particular contexts; that the operating engines behind one's society—including language, politics, and other such broad areas—exist without people having to think about *how* they operate. As an example, how many of us ever question whether the way in which we go about our daily lives is the only (or the best, or a better) way in which to do this? Any reasonable survey of the past, especially one that concentrates on the lives of working people as opposed to a focus on monarchs and other political leaders, makes clear that the way we live today is not the way in which even our direct ancestors lived. And it is more than merely a matter of technological improvements making our world different. To be more specific, why (in America, at least) do we tend to automatically assume that we are entitled to happiness, when history makes clear that the human condition can be a difficult and dangerous one? Why do Americans believe that hard work should equal (material) success, when we know that it is possible to work very hard and not make much money at all? (If you doubt this last comment, consider migrant agricultural workers in the American South and West and ask yourself if you could stoop and pick fruits or vegetables for 12 hours a day for as little as $50.) In some other cultures—Italy and some Latin American countries, for example—hard work is not seen as a necessary component of a "life well lived." Some cultures embrace the essence of the Italian phrase *dolce far niente* (roughly, "it's sweet doing nothing") as the epitome of existence. In this case, working hard at a job to acquire material possessions is considered somewhat foolish, because work gets in the way of relaxation. In our culture, images and stories of how one is *supposed* to act, to look, and to live influence our sense of self and provide patterns for building a way to make meaning of the world.

Ideology

The Bedford Glossary of Critical and Literary Terms defines **ideology** as "a set of beliefs underlying the customs, habits, and practices common to a given social group. To members of that group, the beliefs seem obviously true, natural, and even universally applicable."[13] To reiterate, when the word culture is used in this text, it will often assume and refer to both the actions themselves and to those often-unacknowledged assumptions behind why the action seems right in that group at that time. In other words, ideology is about the belief system. We will discuss the ways in which ideology operates—insofar as groups learn to internalize these belief systems—in later chapters.

The Distinction between High Culture and Popular Culture

When we think about the essence of culture—the act of making meaning from the world—then, we should remember that "culture" does not only refer to the art in museums or to literature, opera, or other so-called examples of "high culture." Americans do not think of themselves as members of a class-conscious society, so the idea of higher- or lower-class cultural activities may seem a bit strange. However, these distinctions, which are remnants of a much stricter hierarchy of classes in European cultures, are still very much in evidence. The difference to our daily lives is that an awareness of class distinctions has faded into the background. Chapter 6 will discuss some of the ways that class status functions in and through language use itself. For our purposes, we need to acknowledge that the word "culture" was originally used in reference to every aspect of the daily lives of all the people who lived in a given place. The phenomenon called globalization has extended the idea of the local in much the same way that the ready availability of print media extended kinship and ethnic groups' control over national units. The spread of printed material after the invention of moveable type by Gutenberg in Europe during the 1400s enabled local groups to spread their cultures beyond the geographic locale in which they lived. In other words, language carries culture.

One generally understood meaning of culture is synonymous with sophistication: you are cultured if you are aware of and schooled in the elements your culture considers to be "sophisticated." If someone takes you to the opera or the theater to see classic dramatic presentations (as opposed to a Broadway viewing of a popular show, which is an example of mass culture), or a symphonic performance (as opposed to a popular band's concert performance), you are being exposed to what is sometimes called "high culture": the art forms of social elites. An **elite**, by definition, is a small, powerful group at the top of a social pyramid. Social elites—including those with a great deal of money—established and maintained cultural standards and norms throughout much of recorded Western history. In the East, Chinese cultural history up until World War II is also the history of the aristocracy and its artistic and cultural activities. In Europe and the United States, social elites—drawing on the rich history of European art, literature, and music—have established a flexible list of "classics" that one must presumably be well educated to enjoy. The power and depth of such classics were long thought to be beyond the ability of ordinary, working people to enjoy. An example of the still-present notion of classic (versus popular) literature can be seen in advertisements such as those for the "world's great books." The appeal made by such marketing claims is to the acquisition of scholarly sophistication: read these texts, such as works by Shakespeare, Cervantes, James Joyce, and others, and you will possess all the literary knowledge you will need to be sophisticated. Own the books—and display them, of course—and you will become part of a cultural elite. Classics are perceived to endure as opposed to "trends" or fads, which come and go because they have no permanent value. A consequence of assuming that there is a central set of texts that convey status (and cultural information) relates to globalization's cultural face: there is the presupposition that "shared" culture will unify and solidify cultural norms. Those who don't read the great books, for example, are kept outside of the halls of cultural power—places like universities and sociopolitical spheres where the insiders share (and assume) a common set of cultural references. Many intellectuals deplore the very idea of classic art, or literature or music, with its claims for the stability of "excellence" over historical time and a lack of concern for those who get to decide what constitutes excellence. Critics of a limited, stable list of unchanging "great works" say that elites perpetuate their own dominance by insisting on criteria that allow their dominance to continue. For such critics the issue is the cultural component and how it operates, not whether it is "serious" or "popular" culture.

If you doubt that social elites can set standards and ostracize those who do not agree with those standards of excellence, consider the cliques of many American high schools and the power elites that control high-school existence. English and American higher education for much of the 20th century was focused upon perpetuating ideas about artistic, literary, and cultural forms; as a result, access to higher education became a pre-condition for sophistication and cultural enlightenment. We can say that an ideology was being formed by this linkage: groups will come to assume that education is a prerequisite for success; their actions will operate in accordance with this set principle.

There have long been those who challenged this elitist notion of culture. American writer Jack London insisted that a common person could exercise his or her intelligence and become a cultural beacon while focusing on working people; noted American poet and teacher Mark Van Doren was another. But it was during the 1960s that literary and art critics began to concentrate on the notion that culture was not only what was studied in museums and in university classrooms. Those who study the various creations of the world without regard to the classic or elite appeal of such creations are generally called **cultural critics**, and they engage in what is generally referred to as cultural studies. The proper field of study for cultural critics is any form of expression within a given society. How one should go about such studies is a matter of some debate, but it will suffice here to say that, very generally, this interdisciplinary area (which can potentially involve one or more elements of social psychology, anthropology, literature, or sociology) is split between ethnographers—people who interview people and extrapolate from this fieldwork—and generalists—who espouse theories and find evidence of those theories in the world.[14] Since we are all exposed to various elements of the social world every day—and because we live our lives under a barrage of images from media and social interactions—simply acknowledging that the concept called culture can be generally defined and studied is a useful start.

Thus, television shows, print and visual media advertisements, comic books, popular music, and so on are all part of what we can broadly refer to as culture. In fact, what we can call **vernacular interaction** (normal, everyday social involvement with others) relies upon such elements to create connections so that a cultural space that includes all adherents can exist. As an example, consider how many times each day you share with peers a knowledge of common cultural events, such as popular music, movies, or television shows. Connections are formed between you and your peers because you share—are bonded by—such shared knowledge. The belief systems of people around the world are made apparent—one group of analysts insists—by examination of the signifying systems they use. A signifying system is a fancy term for a simple concept: a system that contains meaning and thus "signifies" something. An example would be the fashion and fashion commentary one sees in Hollywood awards' ceremonies. The fashion "signifies" in the sense that it conveys a sense of importance to this subculture: those who care about celebrities because they are perceived to have "succeeded" and are thus uniquely qualified to act as models of the culture.

As a vision of culture as one, unified thing has given way to a variety of subcultures—like Goths, skateboarders, business entrepreneurs, hip-hoppers, hippies, academics, and on and on—many cultural critics have turned to examinations of the signifying systems that underlie the expressions of those subcultures. Many of these studies look at the creations (the cultural activities themselves) as evidence of underlying ideologies. Some cultural critics study fashion and popular entertainment. Some study language use in subcultures. Language is an example, a very powerful example, of a signifying system: all the individual elements in the system are interrelated and work in the service of the system as a whole. As we shall see in subsequent chapters, language is a cultural force that unifies people even as it allows for a great deal of variation in the usage of its basic structure.

As a preview of a much longer discussion in Chapter 6, consider the ways in which English operates in your life. Chances are that you are blissfully unaware of most of the rules of grammar and syntax that allow you to converse in your everyday life (much to the chagrin of your English teachers). However, you are quite adept at using the language and are able to do what linguists refer to as code switching, using different styles of speech in different contexts. For example, you are unlikely to converse with your parents and peers using exactly the same vocabulary and register of formality. This difference in the codes used for parents and peers points to the unifying nature of your use of English and to its flexibility at the same time. Haven't you had the experience of having someone from outside of your social group overhear your conversation and comment upon the fact that your speech made little sense to him or her? This text will return to the issue of language and its cultural roles. First, though, we will further explore how culture operates.

American Culture as a Subset of Western Culture

Americans are part of Western culture and thus have inter-nalized a belief in rational, scientific inquiry as a way of understanding the world. Western culture also tends to be characterized by innovation, urbanization, the belief in univer-sal education, and the embrace of individual self-determination. This last core concept is in evidence in the assumption that democratic political structures are perceived to be the natural (almost evolutionary) goal of all societies. We will return to and develop this idea in Chapter 6. American culture is a subset of Western culture, and our core ideals are well established in such documents as the Constitution and Bill of Rights. Most Americans speak English as a primary language, and this differentiates its users from other Western countries where more than one language may customarily be spoken. Among the other distinctions in American culture is a dramatic emphasis on material achievement, an emphasis that is generally, though not universally, shared in European and other world cultures. The region of the country in which you live will also determine subsets, or subcultures, of American culture. Someone raised in rural west Texas, for example, will see things a bit differently—and act, dress and value different things—than someone raised in Brooklyn, New York. Inevitably, you will also share ideological beliefs, of course. Inevitably, "several ideologies may coexist [within a given society]; one or more of these may be dominant."[15] Further subcultures of your cultural membership might include the specific group around you that you emulate. In fact, "ideologies may be forcefully imposed or willingly subscribed to. Their component beliefs may be held consciously or unconsciously."[16] You may or may not know why something is not "cool" or why you wish to act a certain way, but that does not mean that an ideology isn't operating on and through you in the ways you participate in various layers of culture. Obviously, ethnicity and other factors create other cultural preconditions for behavior and the acceptance of behavior.

A more concrete way of looking at the issue lies in actively thinking about why you choose one style of dress or mode of behavior over another. Each of us favors an image of ourselves that announces to the world who we are. Hairstyles, styles of dress and behavior, and language use are examples of choices that are rarely made in a vacuum. We are influenced by styles we admire or that are part of the limited set of models we see, for any of a variety of reasons. In fact, the strength of culture's pull on us all is so powerful that many of the "choices" we make—about dress, speech patterns, or acceptable social behavior, for example—are not really choices at all; rather, it is almost as though we have a limited palette of acceptable choices. Those options that are not acceptable to us are simply off the palette of available options and are never really options at all. It is important to keep in mind, however, that individuals are not puppets, slavishly copying a style/image; people are not simply examples of sociological theories in action.

But people with disposable incomes do provide reasonable markers for general trends that are often given sociological labels. As more options enter the cultural palette—especially as media provide more examples of styles and cultures far from our local spheres of existence—those with the money to experiment become local examples of distant culture, initiating trends that often take hold. An example of the diffusion of style will be developed a bit later in this chapter, when we look at the sub-culture of "Emily the Strange." The point is that the increasing internationalization of otherwise "local" styles provides more possibilities for the exotic to become the norm. Heretofore foreign styles can be more easily viewed and adopted by distant viewers who inhabit a global virtual reality. Throughout this chapter, it will be helpful if you look at the varieties of what we have called subcultures in your own world: what styles tend to predominate? Why are they adopted (or shunned)? Asking questions such as these can help you to use your own experience of culture as a way of accessing the more abstract concepts behind the generality of "culture."

IDENTITY, CULTURAL COMMUNITIES, AND CULTURAL SPACE

Identity is a function of who you are: your sense of yourself, your habits, and turns of mind you have internalized, among many other things. Each of us has an identity. But our identi-ties are in large part a result of our existence within a variety of cultural groups structured around ideological belief systems. Let's examine three dominant kinds of cultural groups (there are others): kinship, ethnic, and national. Imagine three circles: the national circle is the largest; inside of it is the ethnic circle (which often, but not always, includes a religious component); and the smallest, but most integral to the totality of a person's cultural identity, is the circle representing kinship. The most obvious group to which we belong that informs our identity— the most significant cultural group—is kinship. Family mem-bership, including ethnic and religious ties, is what sociologists examine when they examine bonds of kinship. Personal relation-ships and the choices people make for friends would also become part of the kinship relationship. Ethnic cultural relationships include such elements as race, religion, and the implications contained within these broad categories for all other social relationships. Finally, national culture binds members of a very widespread geographic area to each other by virtue of ideology and, often, by very powerful symbolic icons—such as flags or other symbols of national identity.

Nations are not the same as states. A state is a bureaucratic entity that exists to serve a function, like administering laws and doing the business of acting on behalf of its members. As noted earlier, the invention of the printing press in the 15th century created the possibility that ethnic groups could extend their control over much larger areas than had previously been the case. The "nation" and the "state" came together to form the "nation–state" after that period. The countries of Europe, for example, are nation–states. Many of these nation–states have joined an even larger functional bureaucracy (an even larger state)—called the European Union, or the EU—so that state business and economic policy can be conducted more effectively with very large states such as the United States. But the many nations within the EU are still trying to ensure that their national cultures not dissipate in the face of their decision to have a state function that is no longer directly connected to national identity. England's decision to continue to use the British pound (£) rather than the E.U.'s preferred currency, the euro (€) is one simple example of this tension. This is a very important component of globalization, because as noted previously so many of the trends and movements of globalization are trans- national or unaffiliated with a specific nation–state. Also, the notion of some observers that nation-formation will cease in the face of globalization's unifying tendencies has not proved to be true. Ethnic and religious groups in many parts of the world are clamoring for the right of self-determination. It seems likely, for example, that the Kurdish people—whose kinship and ethno- religious cultural bonds span across northern Iraq and southeast- ern Turkey—will continue to cry out for a country of their own.

It bears repeating that culture flows in all directions. People are in motion around the globe in very large numbers at all times. Many are migrating or are forced to flee their home cultures. These groups carry their cultures with them.

Marco Polo and Globalization

The first, great globalizing hero from what is now Europe—Marco Polo—brought back with him from the Chinese emperor Kublai Khan's court a whiff of the exotic (foods, spices, and silks) that constructed an Orientalism (a love of the "other") that has waxed and waned in the West ever since (Figure 3.1). (We will return to the importance of Polo's travels in Chapter 5.) One of the first missionaries to China, Jesuit scholar Matteo Ricci (1552–1610), practically pioneered the Western infatuation with China during the 17th and 18th centuries in Europe. For example, the popularity of a type of porcelain called "blue onion"—which is still manufactured in Germany and has been in continual demand for centuries—is a direct result of missionaries functioning as cultural conduits for style and design from the Far East.

Symbolic and Vernacular Interactions within Cultural Groups

Symbols bind us to people we have never met who are part of our national cultural group. The American flag is a good example of a national cultural symbol. Not everyone within a nation's boundaries is going to agree on the specifics of a given symbol's meaning, but all the members are aware of its power. Pictures of decisive historical events, icons such as George Washington, money, songs, and many other shared elements of national culture help to create unspoken, often unexamined, ties between members in the group. In other words, symbols are examples of a shared ideological bond. The sight of the American flag accompanied by the playing of the "Star-Spangled Banner," the national anthem of the United States, when played to celebrate a gold-medal winner at the Olympics, has different meanings for Americans and Hungarians sitting side by side, watching and listening together.

The vernacular interaction referred to above is even more cohesive in some ways than symbolism. Vernacular means the

Figure 3.1 A miniature painting from Maudeville's *Book of Marvels* depicts Marco Polo being received at the court of Kublai Khan, the founder of the Mongol Dynasty in 13th-century China.

"daily language spoken by everyday people in a given location." Sociologist Martin Spencer calls this type of interaction the recognition of "comfortable communication."[17] Imagine that you are traveling in Asia. You sit at a table in a restaurant with 20 other travelers. You begin talking to a neighbor about football, not realizing that in much of the rest of the world "football" refers to what Americans call soccer. You can certainly communicate, comfortably, but you do not share the many, varied cultural references that would mark you as members of the same culture. When you do meet someone who also belongs to any or all of the three dominant kinds of cultural groups described previously (kinship, ethnic, and national), you inevitably engage in "comfortable communication" without even realizing that this engagement is a cultural phenomenon. Cousins who have never met are able to interact on the basis of family lore. The kinship bond would also include people who come from the same town or attended the same high school. Ethnic cultural bonds can be loosened to include generational and gender-specific touchstones: knowing the same pop song from 30 years ago, having some relationship to a shared group experience (such as having been in the Girl Scouts or having played high-school soccer), and having similar perspectives on historical events. Comfortable conversation does not mean agreement or friendship. It means that you understand each other in a way that is much deeper than simply having many things in common. Those shared commonalities add up to cultural affiliation, that is, membership in a cultural group.

Cultural Space

Depriving cultural groups of a public space to exist, which includes symbolic and vernacular interaction, creates social strife. The conflicts in the former Yugoslavia, waves of ethnic violence in states in Africa, the demands of nation–states within the EU that each be allowed to retain its national identity: all are examples of the fact that cultural space is a contested space. We will use the term **cultural space** to refer to public space that is marked by kinship, ethnic, or national cultural symbolic and vernacular interactions. The two extreme perspectives on globalization's impact that were discussed in Chapter 2 are both heavily invested in the control of cultural space, which includes virtual space such as the Internet and popular media. Those who take the view that globalization is creating a universal cultural reality that goes far beyond the nation–state see positive consequences, such as democratic governance, as a natural outgrowth. Those who oppose globalization's lack of cultural connectedness to kinship, ethnic, and national cultural foundations fear that local cultural realities will wither away in the face of forces tied to global capitalism.

Backlashes against cultural dominance are common. In the Canadian province of Quebec, for example, all official signs must be printed in French to guard against the cultural force of English usage. In the United States, many states have enacted laws proclaiming English as an "official language." As the population density of non-English-speaking cultural groups increases—in places like the southwestern United States and Florida's where Spanish is increasingly spoken—the perceived need to shore up the symbolic and vernacular cultural activities of dominant groups increases tensions between cultural groups.

It is even possible for a constructed, commercial symbol to create cultural ripples, influencing behavior and attracting adherents. By way of illustration, let's explore an example of culture's pull on individual identity even at a distance. This can lead to a better understanding of the interrelationship of cultural activity and globalization's reach.

THE CASE OF EMILY THE STRANGE

In the early 1990s, in an attempt to attract teenaged American girls to its line of clothing, a small, San Francisco-based clothing company, Cosmic Debris, began to hand out stickers with each sale. On the stickers were slogans that celebrated the outsider personality that the clothing was supposed to exhibit. Each sticker had a picture of "Emily," an invented symbol of the line of clothing. She was shown in all her 13-year-old alienation (unsmiling face, jet-black hair, and black clothing) with one or more of her four black cats. These early stickers—and, later, tee shirts, a book, and other extensions of the basic personality—were built around slogans that announced Emily's difference from the norm and thus the clothing's uniqueness and desirability. A typical slogan might read, "Emily didn't search to belong. She searched to be lost."[18] Emily is an example of one type of counterculture: she is against anything the dominant culture sees as important. Her rejection of one cultural pull, however, would come to create a subculture. An explosion of interest and attraction followed on the heels of what was originally a small-scale marketing gimmick, showing the speed with which cultural icons and information can spread. An

Figure 3.2 The home page of *EmilyStrange.com* offers a variety of items, including clothes and accessories that are made available by a San Francisco clothing company called Cosmic Debris. Emily is an example of an imaginary counterculture figure who is opposed to anything in the dominant culture. An Internet search for "Emily the Strange" listed 610,000 sites. The irony of challenging culture by adopting and copying a marketing gimmick is worth considering.

Internet search for the term "Emily the Strange" listed 610,000 sites (Figure 3.2). There are a number of fan-supported websites, including one by 14-year-old Jessica, who reports, "Emily is 13 years old and wicked bad. Bad meaning good. She has a Posse of 4 cats: Miles, Sabbath, Nee Chee, and Mystery. She's really strange and she knows it. She's anticool and doesn't care about what people think of her."[19] Reporting on the growing consumer interest in an icon who "developed" a personality and a personal history in response to the appeal of her alienation, writer Rob Walker noted in the *New York Times* that "The conversion of strangeness to strength has an obvious appeal, which may be why Emily's fan base is widespread and, in some cases, quite devoted. In the fan-tribute section of her Web site is an entry, apparently from a writer in Brazil, signed "Rubia the Strange," accompanied by photos of Rubia's two Emily tattoos."[20]

The company that created Emily now sells more than $5 million of products each year—many of them online—attesting to the desire of many teenagers to display their originality not by *being* original, but by purchasing a concept that promotes individualism. More to the point, the company is no longer in any way in control of the icon or the use to which it is being put: fans build websites and web logs, and eBay auctions sell merchandise. Emily's "culture" has taken on a life of its own, without regard to the intentions of her creators. This is a point that is quite important to an understanding of the globalization of culture: once the information is in circuit, it operates without any necessary connection to its originators.

Emily the Strange speaks to a group that we can label as a subculture because it has organized itself around a concept that helps to give voice to the way the members of the subculture wish to think of themselves as they go about their daily lives. As Rob Walker puts it: "One way to think about any subculture is that it's made up of people who feel strange in more or less the same way. But, of course, if too many people feel strange in the same way, then it's not strange anymore." Walker cites a distressed teenager who bemoans the fact that "all the popular kids like Emily now."[21]

Emily the Strange is an icon, an emblem that is the centralizing focus of what can be seen as a signifying system: the subculture that uses her image to create a composite of what they wish to be, look, and act like. Websites, blogs, e-mail, and more traditional communication forms where those who are "Emily's" can create a subculture complete with slang that excludes those not "in the know" are the arteries and veins through which the creations of this subculture flow. A cultural critic interested in analyzing this subculture would "read" the fashion, mannerisms, slang, and overall activities of the group and come to conclusions about its culture based upon the daily

Headscarves and Cultural Space in France

In September 2004, a French law took effect that required Islamic women to remove their headscarves before entering public schools. The law was not specifically aimed at Islamic culture; the law banned most public displays of religious affiliation. French culture has a long and strict tradition— since the French Revolution in 1789—of separating religious and political activity. In this case, the intent of the law was to curb fundamentalist religious expression in public space. The most publicized implication of the law involved the restriction of Muslim dress. When worn by women raised in Islam, the headscarf is an example of an ethnic cultural symbol that announces religious affiliation with Islam; it can also symbolize kinship relationships as well. One often-stated reason for the ban involved a balance between personal, cultural freedom (the ability to exhibit cultural identity in public by wearing a headscarf), and the need to guarantee public safety by limiting violence against those who display symbols that might be misread by those not in the cultural groups. That members of cultural groups are often viewed stereotypically rather than individually is a hard fact that bears repeating. The French government took this step as a way of controlling its cultural space and as a way of limiting potential incidents against a visible cultural group.

Individual action—in this case a mode of dress—which signals an ethnic (religious) cultural affiliation was perceived to have too great an effect on public space. Individuals can create a "portable cultural space" by the ways in which they dress, speak, act, and so on. In other words, individuals carry and advertise culture and create eddies of cultural activity within the dominant cultural stream of a given public environment. In much the same manner as a young woman wearing a headscarf, the Internet and popular media throughout the world create influence of cultural space, many of which vie for dominance in local environments.

activities of the members of the group. In other words, even people can be seen as "texts" to be read.

Cultural Icons and the Global Marketplace

Phenomena like Emily the Strange can reproduce themselves in the daily activities of individuals around the globe because of the astonishing interconnectedness that communication

France has been torn by a bitter debate over whether Muslim girls should be allowed to wear headscarves in public schools. The separation of religious and political activity has a long history in France, going back to the French Revolution in 1789. This schoolgirl, seen leaving a college in Aubervilliers, a town north of Paris, puts on a headscarf, which announces her religious affiliation with Islam.

Figure 3.3 The designer Michael Lau created a line of action figures based on street culture and hip-hop culture. The first and second 6-inch Gardeners (Tatto) were shown and sold in 1999 at a Michael Lau exhibition in Hong Kong. It would take Michael 2 years before the next 6-inch character was available, but the basis of the collectable Gardeners began here.

technologies allow. In an article that explores a craze of the sort familiar to anyone who knows someone who collects items (baseball or game cards, figurines, etc.) for display and resale, writer Arthur Lubow interviewed Hong Kong designer Michael Lau, who had created a sought-after line of 12-inch action figures modeled after contemporary teenage culture. Hong Kong toy collectors started a craze for the skateboarders, hip-hoppers, and snowboarders Lau had created. Now Lau's action figures sell for hundreds of dollars apiece on eBay auctions (Figure 3.3). The figures illustrate a common truth of culture's global interface.

Lubow quotes Lau describing his inspiration for the dolls: "Street culture and hip-hop culture and skateboard style were coming up . . . . The culture included fashion, music, graffiti. . . . It is just like a uniform—people in Hong Kong and Tokyo and Britain and the States all look the same." The baggy shorts, tent-like sweaters, chains, earrings, and tattoos all speak to a globally identifiable culture with tendrils in every part of the world with access to media.[22] As John Tomlinson puts it in his discussion of globalization's cultural component:

> . . . we are concerned with . . . how globalization alters the context of meaning construction: how it affects people's sense of identity, the experience of place and of the self in relation to place, how it impacts on the shared understandings, values, desires, myths, hopes, and fears that have developed around locally situated life.[23]

Ultimately, each of us has an identity that is formed by the intersection of kinship, ethnic, and national cultural realities. Additionally, global economic activity creates other cultural models, as the Internet and international media make certain images powerful players in societies around the world. In fact, as we are increasingly bombarded with images and symbols, we change—sometimes without really knowing why. Culture is a force with many layers, and our individual identities are bound to the influences that culture's many pulls exert on us. We will examine the term cultural imperialism, a term crucial to the understanding of globalization and culture, in Chapter 6. **Cultural imperialism** refers to the way that the culture of a dominant group can overpower the culture of a previously distinct cultural group. Prior to that discussion, however, we need to explore two other issues: imperialism, or the growth of empires, in general and the power of language as it shapes our thinking.

The Pre-History
of Globalization

The control of cultural space and the imposition of a dominant culture—by either coercive or indirect means—is central to an understanding of the history of the last several thousand years. Globalization is a newer example of an ancient phenomenon, made more dynamic due to the speed with which culture can spread across the globe. Some scholars link imperial growth—nation–states' control of far-flung colonies—and by extension globalization with market forces: Natural resources move from and capital investment flows to underdeveloped parts of the world. Further, people move from and to imperial, industrial and financial centers of power. American culture is often seen as the same as globalization's cultural face, which is obviously overstating the case. As we shall see in subsequent chapters, however, the force of American popular culture is powerful and very evident in almost every part of the world.

But before rushing to any conclusions about the unquestioned dominance of American cultural icons such as Ronald McDonald or Britney Spears, it is worth remembering two facts: first, cultural flow works in all directions (not just from America to the rest of the world, but from the rest of the world to the rest of the world); second, although the speed of modern telecommunications makes the spread of cultural information in all media lightning fast, history is filled with examples of large-scale fascination with the new and exotic.

Literature in the Imperial Court of Heian Japan

In the 7th century, a Japanese delegation to the imperial court in China was so overawed by what they heard, saw, and experienced that they returned home to Japan with tales of a superior culture. The Japanese would spend the next several hundred years building a civilization that was in many ways a mirror of Chinese culture. The Imperial Court of the Heian Period in Japan was a slavish copy of the Chinese model: Chinese (not Japanese) was the language of educated, sophisticated aristocrats; a court bureaucracy identical to the civil service of Chinese invention was put into place; and almost all cultural forms (poetry, painting, architecture, dress, and decor) were copied from the Chinese. Only women wrote in the vernacular (everyday) language of the Japanese people.

In the 10th and 11th centuries, it was Japanese women— including Sei Shonagon and Lady Murasaki Shikibu,— who would write their observations of the Heian Court and in the process establish a national literature by their avoidance of the dominant Chinese cultural influence. The works of these writers, including *The Pillow Book* and *The Tale of Genji*, constitute the beginnings of native Japanese prose (Figure 4.1).

The tension between the power of external, dominant cultural forces and local, "native" practices is at the heart of culture's

Figure 4.1 *The Tale of Genji,* written by Lady Murasaki Shikibu in the 11th century, is acknowledged as the first Japanese prose classic. Writing in the common language of her day, she helped to establish a national literature. The work traces the life of Prince Genji, his wives and children, and the complex fictional life they lived. The painting depicts scene 54 from the scroll of *The Tale of Genji.*

relationship to globalization. Cultural conflict is timeless, and it is valuable to examine some broad tendencies in past eras of empire and influence, especially insofar as language use is involved.

WHY THE PRE-HISTORY OF GLOBALIZATION MATTERS
Although many people think of the late 20th century when they think of globalization, the reality is that world history is a series of attempts to create a single, integrated, and interdependent

world. This core definition of globalization will remind the reader that the presumably separate fields of economics (trade and commerce), language, culture, and politics are very much interrelated. In fact, even historical studies of the interconnections between native groups in the Americas before Christopher Columbus arrived underline this fact. One prominent professor of anthropology, Eric R. Wolf, notes that interconnectedness—not groups developing in isolation—was the norm:

> Everywhere in this world of 1400, populations existed in interconnections. Groups that defined themselves as culturally distinct were linked by kinship or ceremonial allegiance; states expanded, incorporating other peoples into more encompassing political structures; elite groups succeeded one another, seizing control of agricultural populations and establishing new political and symbolic orders. Trade formed networks from East Asia to the Levant, across the Sahara, from East Africa through the Indian Ocean to the Southeast Asian archipelago.[24]

In other words, the world—even in the year 1400, even in the world not yet "discovered" by Europe—was already exhibiting connections that we can recognize as related to the idea of globalization, the movement toward an integrated and interdependent world. Most of us have some sense of the growth and decline of ancient empires such as those of Greece and Rome, or of the colonial expansion that marked Spanish and English imperial activities. Even the immense Chinese empire, the Qing—which controlled a very large expanse of Asia through the end of the 19th century—provides a template for understanding unification and centralized control over various cultural groups. Interdependence and interconnections were not unique to the "old" worlds of Europe and Asia, however. As Wolf has noted:

> Conquest, incorporation, recombination, and commerce also marked the New World. In both hemispheres populations

impinged upon other populations through permeable social boundaries, creating intergrading, interwoven social and cultural entities. If there were any isolated societies these were but isolated phenomena—a group pushed to the edge of a zone of interaction and left to itself for a brief moment in time.[25]

This chapter will explore the fact that there have been other situations in history that are related to the tendency toward global unity. In at least one case, technological breakthroughs helped to allow one culture to impose its will, its language, and its culture on others. In the past, such empire building led to historical horrors such as the slave trade, colonialism, and the oppression of indigenous populations throughout the world. The late-20th-century phenomenon referred to as globalization is a web of economic, political, linguistic, and cultural effects enabled by advances in communications technology and led by the development of computer chips. There have been at least two other times in history when culture, language, and economics combined to create a movement toward what can be called a global state. The first is the spread of the Roman Empire; the second is the growth of British imperial dominion.

A technological innovation—the printing press, and the subsequent distribution of large numbers of books written in vernacular languages—led to the disintegration of a culture unified by the use of Latin as an official language. For almost 1,700 years, the official language—of the legal system, of diplomacy, and of all court documents—was Latin, a version of the language spoken by the Romans from about 400 B.C. to about 750 A.D.

The growth of the British Empire, from about 1600 A.D. through the early 20th century, is intricately connected to the imposition of a common language (English) and the cultural consequences forced upon native peoples by that imposition. Further, technological developments—notably, those related to developments in navigation and communications—allowed the British to control trade in distant parts of the globe. In both the Roman and British cases, economics, language, culture, and politics were intertwined in ways that make an understanding of these precursors important to an understanding of the globalization movement in the late 20th century.

THE ROMAN EMPIRE AND THE SOCIAL TRIUMPH OF THE CHRISTIAN CHURCH

At the height of its power, a Roman citizen could travel from what is now southern England to almost Afghanistan knowing that wherever he went, he would be understood (Figure 4.2). He could converse in Latin to local, Roman-appointed officials throughout the empire, confident that knowledge of this universal language would speed his journey—regardless of the language(s) spoken by indigenous groups. Even after an attack on Rome itself by the Visigoth leader Alaric in August of 410 A.D., Latin continued to hold sway as the key language of all of Europe and much of the Middle East. As proof of its power as social currency, just four years after Alaric's sack of Rome, a 40-year-long translation project came to an end when the Hebrew *Bible* was translated into Latin by an ascetic scholar named Jerome. Edward Gibbon, who published the influential but controversial *Decline and Fall of the Roman Empire* in 1776, the same year that the British empire was challenged by the American Declaration of Independence (1776), remarked that even barbarians with contempt for Rome and Latin "were ambitious of conversing in Latin, the military idiom of even the Eastern empire."[26] For Gibbon, as for many others, "language was the leading principle which unites or separates the tribes of mankind."[27]

The story of the growth and decline of Rome is still a source of debate among scholars. The causes behind the eventual dissipation of the military power of Rome and its subsequent transformation into the Catholic Church's control over European institutions for 1,000 years include sources of disagreement over trade and political policies. For example, many of the barbarian

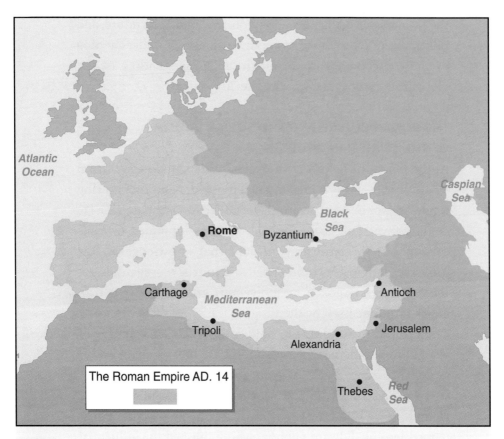

Figure 4.2 The reach of the Roman Empire was from southern England to almost Afghanistan. The power of Rome's cultural reach is still evident today; Latin is one of the linguistic foundations for modern English.

tribes who spent decades bringing the Roman Empire to an effective end in the 5ᵗʰ century A.D. had been mercenaries, people hired to fight for another country than their own, protecting Rome's borders. For our purposes, we merely need to observe that the power of Rome's cultural reach continues to our own day, not least in the fact that Latin is one of several linguistic foundations for modern English.

But Rome did fail, and the various barbarian tribes that scoured Europe, Western Asia, and Northern Africa from about 370 to 630 A.D.—the Visigoths, the Huns, the Vandals, and others—failed to create a replacement "empire." The control of Europe's culture would ultimately rest with the Catholic Church, and its sway—also linked to control of information—would grow and tighten in the form of the Holy Roman Empire, which consisted of many of the countries of Western and Central Europe. After the Battle of Jena (1806), in which Napoleon decisively defeated Prussia (part of what is now Germany), Napoleon effectively abolished the Empire. The year 1806 is a reasonable marker for the effective end of the Holy Roman Empire, though certainly not for the end of the influence of the Roman Catholic Church. It is not overstating the case to say that some of the tensions in the world today are by-products of the conflict between competing ideologies—such as religion. To ignore the unifying control of Christianity in the 1,400 years after the fall of Rome is to ignore one foundational, cultural reality of our world today.

Emperor Constantine and the Triumph of the Ancient Church

It is not normally the case that students of history can point to one day as a hinge for a significant cultural shift. However, there is one such day that helps to show the moment when Christianity became the ultimate successor of the empire of Rome. On October 28th, 312 A.D., at a bridge in Italy, the eventual Emperor of the Byzantine Empire (centered in what is now Turkey) defeated a Roman general and declared himself master of the whole Roman west. Constantine's victory at the Milvian Bridge ended a period of crisis between the eastern and western arms of the Roman Empire. Before the pitched battle began, Constantine proclaimed to his generals that he had had a vision. He had dreamed that a voice demanded that he paint a symbol representing Jesus Christ on the shields of his soldiers if he wished to win the day. Although they were heavily outnumbered, Constantine's troops—with the two Greek letters symbolizing Christ on their

shields—defeated the troops of the Roman general
Maxentius and guaranteed that the Roman Empire
would henceforth be controlled from Constantinople.

Of even greater significance was that Constantine's
vision (and victory) made him a convert to Christianity,
guaranteeing that the Roman Empire would henceforth
be an empire inextricably linked to the Catholic Church.
What had begun as a marginalized—indeed, a persecuted—
religious ideology became the central doctrine of a
political empire. This metaphor of the transfer of
imperial control (though far from complete) can also
be seen as one way of understanding the continuing
conflict, newly born in incidences of international
terrorism on behalf of fundamentalist religious adherents,
between segments of the Islamic world and the heirs of
the Christian/Roman empires.

COERCIVE VERSUS INDIRECT CULTURAL CONTROL

Roman administrators in far-flung districts (or in Rome itself)
did not care whether the people they ruled were acculturated in
Roman beliefs and culture. The Roman world relied upon a slave
economy: only Roman citizens had any real freedom. Coercion
and repression of any threat to a Roman citizen or to Rome itself
was instantly and harshly visited upon any person or group
that expressed disagreement with the way things were. Roman
ideology was imposed from above—coercively. People were
forced to obey by law and force of arms.

There are two basic ways to get people to do what you want
them to do: make them (coerce them) or convince them to
believe that what you want done is the "right" thing to do. We
can refer to these two methods as coercion and immersion.
Recall that ideology can be apparent to those who ascribe to it
or invisible to its adherents. Ideological control is strongest
when the principles that govern action are internalized by
cultural groups as the normal way of things. As we have seen,

culture's powerful effects can often leave us blind to the assumptions that underpin our judgment.

BRITISH IMPERIAL CONTROL

While over its long history the British Empire committed its share of repressive acts, the British also used a form of ideological indoctrination of its subjects that influenced them—by immersion, not coercion—to consider themselves linked to the goals and needs of the British Empire. Rarely entirely complete, the more indirect method sought to create cultural bonds between rulers and the ruled.

This indirect form of ideological control is often called the subaltern system. Rather than rule directly, administrators in the British colonies of India and elsewhere would train subalterns, or local subordinates, to administer everyday control over their own people. The net effect of this type of ideological control is actually much more insidious and powerful than its more direct

A Snapshot of Ideological Coercion in the Roman Empire

Using one 30-year-long period in Rome's history (from 150 to 120 B.C.), we can use four brutal events to illustrate the repression that Rome visited on any who questioned its ideological and political dominance or stood in its way.

In 146 B.C., Rome crushed a revolt in Greece. Rome razed the city of Corinth, killing all the men and selling all of the women and children into slavery. In 132 B.C., 20,000 slaves were crucified on the island of Sicily, a savage end to a 3-year-long slave revolt. In 133, an aristocrat, Tiberius Gracchus, and 300 of his followers who had agitated for land reform were assassinated. This put an end to a movement that had called for a redistribution of land ownership in favor of plebeians—non-aristocrats. In 123 B.C., Roman General Quintus Fabius Maximus received a triumph, featuring a monumental parade through Rome, for his bloody defeat of a large army of tribesmen in southern Gaul (in what is now France). Maximus's victory created access to fertile farmland that helped defuse the continuing demand for land redistribution.

repressive counterpart. By indoctrinating people who generally looked like, acted like, and believed in the same things as those who needed to be "ruled," British colonial administrators in India, Africa, and elsewhere were able to appear (relatively) benevolently authoritarian even as the subalterns acted as policemen, postal workers, and even soldiers in the more direct repression of their own peoples.

It is incorrect to assume, however, that ideological control was complete or even that it worked. The net effect of collaboration was all that was required. As one historian puts it:

> Faced with the onward march of British imperialism and European civilization, local peoples had to make a choice between acceptance and defiance, collaboration and resistance. It is small wonder that for the most part collaboration with the imperial authorities became the inevitable consequence of imperial expansion and control. Without the collaboration—or at any rate the acquiescence—of local elites, tribal and religious groupings, the different castes and subdivisions of colonial society, the British would never have been able to carry out their stupendous task of conquering, ruling, dominating, and controlling so large a proportion of the planet. [28]

By the start of the 20th century, Britain controlled almost one-quarter of the world's surface area (Figure 4.3). The power of the English navy and the rapid spread of technologies controlled by Europeans—such as the steamship, railroad, and telegraph—allowed this far-flung empire to exist in a meaningful way for almost 200 years. There were constant reminders of revolution from "below," as native peoples in Africa and India attempted to overthrow their rulers, but the British Empire was still a reality until after World War II.

A seminal event occurred in the "jewel" of the empire, India, in 1835, when English became the official language of instruction in that country. This was a self-conscious effort to acculturate

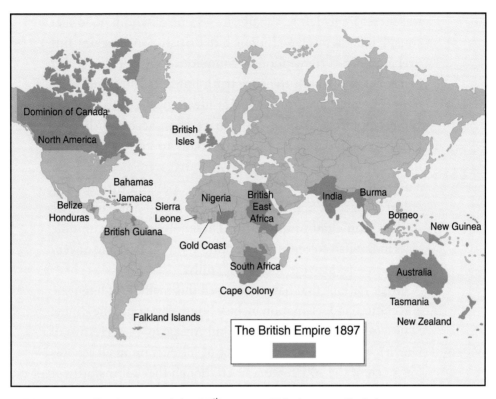

Figure 4.3 By the start of the 20th century, Britain controlled almost one-quarter of the world's surface. Although there were efforts at revolution from below, particularly in India and Africa, the British Empire was still a reality until after World War II.

Indians (who spoke Hindi and many other languages) into British culture by controlling their language. A variant of this policy was followed throughout English colonies in Africa, with the added wrinkle that many of the schools were run, initially, by Christian missionaries. Access to any education at all made one an experiment in ideological indoctrination.

Prior to 1835, subcontinent Indians who were able to go to school had been trained in Sanskrit, Persian, and even Arabic. The "immersion-effect" worked for the English, as generations of Indians became able to staff the bureaucracy in India. Although ultimate control and nearly all policy decisions resided in the hands of Englishmen, the actual running of the country was increasingly left to subalterns—some of whom no longer considered themselves Indian but British. Once again, this oversimplifies a tremendously complicated set of cultural and historical events, but the core truth holds: cultural indoctrination created a more complete ideological control over a subject population than could have been accomplished by purely coercive means. Limiting access to education was a means of limiting access to the jobs that were necessary for existence in a cash economy. Without passing through the cultural space of English ideology, one could not participate in the colonial administration. These jobs created a middle class in English colonies and became a way—often one of very few ways—to provide for one's family.

Other nations that have since used this method of linguistic and cultural indoctrination include South Africa and the United States. In South Africa, English and Afrikaans (a derivative of Dutch) were the official languages of instruction in all schools for much of the 20th century, even though the vast majority of the population spoke one of nine other languages as a primary language. In the United States, the federal government in the 19th century created Indian boarding schools (a notable one was in Carlisle, Pennsylvania) that insisted that Native Americans— forced away from their homes and into these schools—give up their languages and speak only English.

In the next chapter we will begin a discussion of the power of the "mind-map" that is language. We turn, in Chapter 6, to the intersections of language, culture, and politics. Throughout, we will return to the examples and ideas treated in the first four chapters.

Maps and Language

"On one thing the whole world seems to agree: Globalization is homogenizing cultures. At least a lot of countries are acting as if that's the case."[29]

—Tyler Cowen

In reality, not everyone would agree with Professor Cowen's belief that cultural homogenization is inevitable. As we observed in Chapter 1, globalization's pressure on cultures around the world is undeniable, but by no means absolute. Still, we acknowledged that the beginning of understanding would come with a model that is limited if oversimplified. The case of the Treaty of Tordesillas links together a variety of seemingly unconnected topics: geographic mapping, language use, the authority of certain languages, the tendency of unity and division to exist simultaneously, and most important the lasting consequences of mapping and language use on political and cultural events. The language one uses can be considered as a sort of a map that the mind uses to process the input the world offers, so understanding that maps (and therefore languages) have limitations is an important step toward understanding the tension between a movement toward global unity and the tendency to fragmentation that opposes that movement.

An additional example—a more modern version of the Treaty of Tordesillas—can be seen in the consequences of an 1884 gathering of European leaders called the Berlin Congress. The leaders of 14 European countries met to set guidelines for the colonial "claiming" of African territories. The participants were, in a way, the forefathers of a group referred to as the G8 countries, because they assumed—like the Pope in 1494—that economic control and political dominance could be asserted from afar. Once again, Portugal was involved in the activity: Portugal urged German Chancellor Otto von Bismark to call the conference in 1884. After the Berlin Congress, the template for the colonial "scramble for Africa" was set. Africa's many political and cultural problems for the past 100+ years are easily related to the fact that European powers decided among themselves which territories would be controlled by which European countries. Prior to the Congress, "80% of Africa remained under traditional and local control."[30] The Congress of Berlin calls to mind the Treaty of Tordesillas: leaders of European countries participated in cartographic division of a world that they did not inhabit but wished to control. The realities of the people who lived in South America and Africa were irrelevant to the discussions of those who mapped spheres of influence in what they perceived as the centers of their worlds—in languages that bespoke power and uniformity (Latin for the Pope; French for the diplomats in Berlin).

In other words, following up on the quote at the start of this chapter, globalization—the spread of economic markets as they integrate communities throughout the world—is led by the globalization of culture, especially that of Western culture. One well-known cultural critic, Fredric Jameson, summarizes the dangers of a "one-world" view: "the standardization of world culture, with local popular culture or traditional forms driven out or dumbed down to make way for American television, American music, food clothes, and films, has been seen by many as the very heart of globalization."[31] The movement towards a unified world culture—an illusion, according to many—is opposed by a corresponding movement in favor of local cultures. Those who oppose the homogenization of the world's cultures by the spread of Western (and especially American) culture are opposed by many others who observe that homogeneity (sameness) and heterogeneity (diversity) are able to operate at the same time—often to the mutual benefit of both local and world culture.[32] Using maps as an analogy for how language operates can help to explain this tension.

   We all tend to view the world as centered on ourselves. Thus, each of us highlights our concerns and our way of looking at the larger world through the lens of our local and personal filters. While this might seem obvious, have you ever considered the possibility that your native language creates a filter that skews your view of how the world operates? Here is where the visual nature of geographic maps can help. The map shown in Figure 5.1 is a modern redrawing of the famous Mercator projection that many students in America used up until the 1980s as their reference for how the world "looks." A reproduction of the original map, for navigation by sea, can be seen in Figure 5.2.

   Notice the fact that the "boxes" that describe the intersecting lines of latitude (east–west lines) and longitude (north–south lines) become more rectangular as one nears the polar regions. This is especially clear in Figure 5.1. The effect of this distortion—which makes geographical elements nearer the poles seem much larger than they actually are—is a common problem in mapmaking. The world is, of course, a sphere, a three-dimensional figure. Maps are two-dimensional representations of that three-dimensional reality. As an example of what happens when you try to translate three dimensions into two dimensions, take an orange and draw a series of pictures all over the outer skin with a black marker. Now take the skin off the orange and try to lay out the skin on a flat surface

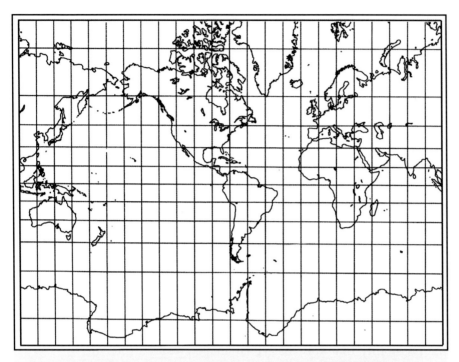

Figure 5.1 This is a modern redrawing of the 1569 map on which
Gerardus Mercator introduced his famous projection. The rectangles that
form a grid from north to south are longer as they move toward the North
and South Pole. This makes the geographic elements nearer the poles
seem larger than they actually are.

so that you can read the pictures in their precise relationship to the
original drawings you made on the surface of the three-dimensional
orange. Nigel Holmes, mapmaker for *Time* magazine, writes, 'The
peel won't lie flat. Map projection is the science of wrestling the
orange peel into submission.'"[33] The inevitable result is some
distortion: flattening a sphere into a "projection" of that sphere
that can be seen in two dimensions (like in a book) means that you
sacrifice either the relative sizes of elements in their relations to
one another or the shapes of the things themselves.

Mapmakers have always struggled with this problem, and it
is not really an issue as long as one understands the central reality of mapmaking: that "every map is a purposeful selection from
everything that is known, bent to the mapmaker's ends. Every

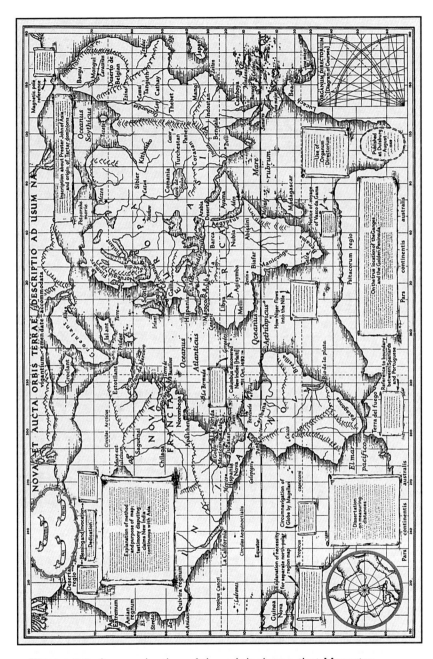

Figure 5.2 A reproduction of the original map that Mercator published in 1569. It was called "A new and enlarged description of the Earth with corrections for use in navigation" and presented a new projection.

map serves a purpose. Every map advances an interest."[34] Too often, however, we develop a mindset based upon how we think the world "looks." Just like the vision of New York City as seen in the *New Yorker* cartoon that viewed the United States from the perspective of New Yorkers: Only those points of interest to New Yorkers appear and the rest of the country is foreshortened. Maps are, themselves, instruments that aid in any of a variety of tasks: navigation, population studies, economic growth, and so on. But every selection of some elements involves suppressing others. For example, a map that is made to show the distribution of languages around the world would select languages and possibly the numbers of people in countries that speak them; the mapmakers would not need to pay attention—they would suppress—the need to illustrate precise details about coastlines, the relative sizes of the geographical elements on the map, and so on. Maps are representations that serve a purpose, nothing more or less. In Figure 5.3, you can see another version of the Mercator map. Notice the relative sizes of Europe and South America, both darkened for ease of comparison. In Figure 5.4, a map that shows the actual relative sizes of the continents (but that distorts their shapes) can be seen. This map, called the Peters projection, shows the relative sizes of Europe and South America in their true relationship. It may come as a surprise to some that North America, and the United States in particular, is not as large as you might think it should be. But this mapping is an accurate representation of the relative sizes of all landmasses. It is not "more right" than the Mercator projection; it simply serves a different purpose. It is possible that some people might be vaguely troubled by seeing the world in this way—as if size devalued the relative importance of a culture or a nation.

Now let's take it a step further. Is North America really on the "left" side of the world? We read in English, so we automatically go to the top, left-hand side of a new page to begin reading or looking. There is nothing "natural" about this automatic move:

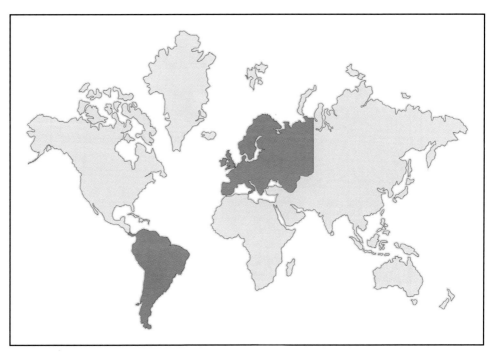

Figure 5.3 This is another version of the Mercator projection that makes Europe appear larger than South America even though South America is 3.1 million square miles larger in area. Maps are representations that are created to serve a purpose rather that to reflect "reality."

it is a product of our acculturation, how we are taught. Not all languages have this automatic orientation. The top, left-hand portion of a map will be a special position—one of importance—for those taught to read in English. If you are raised to speak (and read) in Hebrew, however, your eye will tend to track to the top, right-hand side of a page, because Hebrew readers read from right to left. Other languages have other "automatic-scrolling" start points: many Asian languages, for example, read top-to-bottom, beginning also at the top left. A final assumption of most of the maps we are presented with is the north–south orientation of the world. The idea of "north" is a convenient fiction, because the world as seen from outer space does not present itself in conformity with our sense of north and south poles.[35]

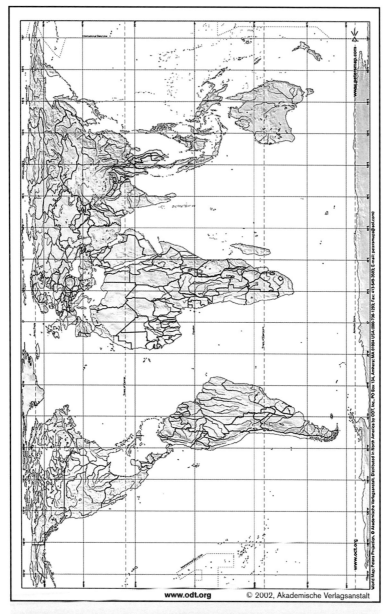

Figure 5.4 This Peters World Map shows the relative sizes of South America and Europe in their true relationship. You can now easily see that South America is much larger than Europe. This map shows the accurate representations of the relative sizes of all landmasses. It is not more correct than the Mercator projections shown before; it simply serves a different purpose.

The point of these illustrations and examples is this: the language you were raised in becomes something of a baseline for how you see the world. There are many unconscious assumptions that go along with your native language. If English is seen as the language of globalization—the unifying cable that carries the homogenizing economic, cultural, and social tendencies some critics worry about—it is important to look at the cultural assumptions behinds English as a globalizing phenomenon. English is a map that is imprinted on the mind in much the same way that our view of the world is imprinted on us by the maps we have seen. Of course, there are limitations to this analogy, as Chapter 6 will discuss. The next step is to look at how English operates and see what sorts of overt and unconscious assumptions are related to language and culture.

LANGUAGE AS A MAP

If one recognizes the limited but very real value of maps as a way to understand the world, it is possible to see that the map one constructs of the world can lead to a foundation for viewing everything in that world. For example, if you are raised to believe that the Earth is the center of the universe, then your understanding of the relative importance of everything in the universe is predetermined by that belief. In the same way, the "map" of the world you have in your mind is a result of the maps you have been shown over the course of your lifetime. If you have not seen a map like the Peters projection, then how could you possibly come to question the relative accuracy of maps like Mercator's? Again, recall that maps are always purpose-driven: Mercator's projection was designed for navigational purposes, and it fulfills that purpose beautifully. However, it necessarily distorts the relative sizes of landmasses in fulfilling its purpose.

Although few languages are "designed" and built for specific purposes, the primary language that you have learned to speak acts like a sort of map in your mind. If you only speak one language, then you understand the world as it filters through your perception in that language. Linguistics is the study of how languages operate. Some linguists study how languages have developed over time, and others study how languages function at a given moment in time. In general, linguists can be divided into two camps. One set believe, following a very famous scientist named Karl Wilhelm von Humboldt (see box in Chapter 6), that the "language that you speak governs all of your perceptions." These theorists believe in the relative autonomy of language and culture. In other words, language is a tool that can be used "outside" of who we are as humans. The other, competing camp, which includes such noted linguistic theorists as Noam Chomsky, believes that there is a fundamental commonality that unites all of the world's many languages. These theorists believe that there is a universal foundation that allows for complete translation. As Professor Bruce Robbins of Columbia University puts it,

> Modern linguistics continues to split sharply between Humboldtians who believe in linguistic relativity and anti-Humboldtians (including artificial intelligence specialists) who believe in a common basis for language that allows for an ideal of perfect equivalence and translation among them.[36]

Robbins is underlining a key point here: If there is an ultimate, innate, commonly shared "language instinct," then humans can move easily between cultural (language-based) experiences. If, on the other hand, language is "relativistic" (specific to the cultural groups that use a given language), then each language or cultural group operates in ways that disallow "perfect" understanding.

We will continue this focus in Chapter 6, where the issue of linguistic relevance will be more sharply defined. As an extension of the ideas presented in this chapter, it is worth looking briefly at "the efficacy of literature as a medium of cultural contact."[37] In other words, how do acts of language, like literature, affect cultures at a distance?

The Novel as a Map of Cultural Activity

Literary critics have long recognized the role of women in the dissemination and growth of the novel. Novels describe the everyday activities of people—usually people excluded from other genres. As a result, the novel form is uniquely suited to a discussion of culture as it crosses boundaries of national and ethno-religious boundaries. Novelists such as Miguel de Cervantes, whose *Don Quixote*, published in 1605, is arguably the first modern European novel, and Gustave Flaubert, whose classic text, *Madame Bovary*, published in 1857, sketched the danger of believing that fictional texts are valid models for life. In *Madame Bovary*, for example, a woman ends up committing suicide because the actions she had attempted in her search for a more "novelistic" (that is, narratively exciting) existence were thwarted. In *Don Quixote*, the knightly protagonist's delusions develop out of his too-literal belief that the courtly adventures he had read are the way that life should be.

In the 10th and 11th centuries, Japanese women, writing in the vernacular Japanese, basically established a national literature. Lady Murasaki's *The Tale of Genji* is generally acknowledged as the first true Japanese prose classic. Some go so far as to consider it the first novel. More generally, the creation of a literate population in the European 19th century led to the rise of the popular literary form of the novel that we know today. Many of the most popular American novelists of the 19th century were women (including Louisa May Alcott and Harriet Beecher Stowe), though their texts were considered "merely popular" reading, not "literature." ("Those damned women scribblers," as Nathaniel Hawthorne called them, irked by the popularity of their novels.) The distinction between high and low culture can help to understand how this might, then, have been an ideology in the ascendancy. Not all narratives are novels, but it helps to think "novelistically" when thinking about cultural contact because we describe the world in language, of course, but also in stories.

The most influential narrative of Europe in the late 13th century is also a text of some interest to students of globalization. *Il Milione*, Marco Polo's travel memoir (which is undeniably fictional in many of its elements) described Kublai Khan at the height of his imperial power as he wielded influence over China and a far-flung empire:

> The encounter between Kublai Khan and Marco Polo is one of the most remarkable stories about the origin of globalization and the role of literature as a medium of cultural contact. As the founder of the Mongol dynasty in 13th-century China and unparalleled patron of Chinese literature and culture, Kublai Khan was also one of the first and greatest imperial minds. His colonial interests led him into many disastrous foreign expeditions beyond the sea. . . . He chose foreigners from Turkistan, Persia, Armenia, and Byzantium as ministers, generals, governors, envoys, astronomers or physicians, and invited Marco Polo, traveling adventurer from Italy, to pass many years in his service.[38]

Professor Gabriele Schwab at the University of California at Irvine makes a modern connection with this ancient story, quoting a particular encounter between Polo and the great Khan as they pore over a map of the world that serves as central anecdote in 20th-century Italian novelist Italo Calvino's novel of cultural fragmentation, *Invisible Cities*:

> The Great Khan owns an atlas whose drawings depict the terrestrial globe all at once and continent by continent, the borders of the most distant realms, the ships' routes, the coastlines, the maps of the most illustrious metropolises and the most opulent ports. . . . The atlas depicts cities which neither Marco nor the geographers know exist or where they are . . . cities that do not have a form or a name . . . In the last pages of the atlas there is an outpouring of networks without

beginning or end, cities in the shape of Los Angeles, in the shape of Kyoto–Osaka, without shape.[39]

Calvino presents what we will come to call a postmodern effect, one that stresses a geography of the mind. For our purposes at this moment, the central importance is to recognize that Polo's encounter, fictionalized by Calvino, becomes a way of seeing that Polo's

> late-13th-century document [*Il Milione*] was to become a model for colonial travel narratives during the so-called discovery of the New World and shaped the Western cultural imaginary with its Orientalist phantasms and its fascination with the marvels of foreign worlds. *Il Milione* made its impact on 15th-century geographical, ethnological, and cosmographic conceptions. . . . Columbus carried a carefully annotated copy of the manuscript with him on his journeys."[40]

Maps, then, have imaginative potential, whether they are cartographically accurate or imaginatively conceived. The map in the mind that is language creates a geography of the imagination, one that potentially prestructures our experiences of the world.

Language, Culture, and Politics

Although it oversimplifies a large number of controversial issues in linguistics, the idea that language use creates a map in the mind that filters experience is a useful one, as long as we don't press the issue too far. The linguistic filter that is language—our mind map, if you will— acts as an interface for our understanding of the world. Further, language and culture are inextricably linked. Chapter 3 introduced some concepts concerning culture that are worth recalling here: personal identity is not something that we create out of thin air, but is a result of such cultural "pulls" as language, ethnicity, kinship, and nationality. As James Hurford, a professor of linguistics at Edinburgh University, has said, "Human languages, such as French, Cantonese or American Sign Language, are socio-cultural entities. Knowledge of them ('competence') is acquired by exposure to the appropriate environment. Languages are maintained and transmitted by acts of speaking and writing; and this is also the means by which languages evolve."[42] We do not, initially, have much choice in deciding what our personal identity will be, although our individual psychological make-up is also involved. We are cultural beings who express ourselves in certain ways, and believe in certain things, due to the effects of culture upon us. Some psychologists have gone so far as to suggest that even the psychosocial development of individuals is a function of external (that is, cultural) forces. This chapter will examine various ways in which language operates as a cultural force, allowing for and at the same time limiting our belief systems (our ideological assumptions). First, though, a qualification of the degree to which "language structures thought and reality" is in order.

COMPETING CONCEPTIONS OF LANGUAGE

Is language (whether English, Mandarin, Tamil, Spanish, or American Sign Language) a tool outside of us that we use and discard—and is therefore unrelated to who we are and how we think and act? Or does language help construct the way we see the world? This second question raises the issue of whether a person raised in a given language experiences the world—and conveys expressions consistent with those experiences—in ways different from a person raised in a different language. As we shall see, this view is called linguistic relativism; although there are "families of languages," the relative differences between languages resist the notion that there is a point at which all languages are the same—a linguistic universalism into which we can tap at will. Figure 6.1 illustrates one section of what is commonly called the "tree of languages" as they developed over time. It shows that modern English—in its many dialectical forms, such as those used by American, British, Spanish, Chinese, or Malaysian speakers—derives from a "root" that also led to the evolution of Latinate and Germanic languages.

Although there are historical relationships apparent between, say, German and English, the wide variations in the way subgroups

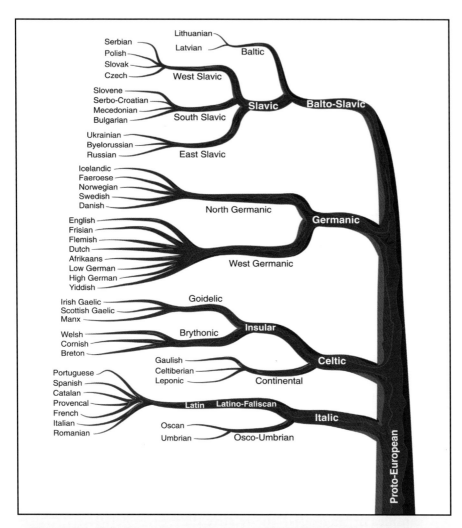

Figure 6.1 This figure illustrates one section of what is commonly called the "tree of languages," as they developed over time. It shows that modern English derives from a "root" that also led to the Latin and Germanic languages.

of these large categories use a given language create problems of understanding even within the language group itself. When one assumes that concepts and abstractions can be perfectly accommodated as "transferable" between language groups, one is assuming a troubling linguistic universalism. In other words, "perfect translations" of one language into another are extremely unlikely. As linguist Michelle Fram-Cohen stated in a 1985 essay entitled "Language, Reality, Translation," "The field of translation is in an awkward situation. Works of translation are carried out while most linguistic theories are skeptical about their possibility to be carried out."[43]

The first question asked at the beginning of this chapter leads to an avenue of inquiry that most linguistic theorists and cultural anthropologists would agree is worth pursuing: the ability to learn language is (with few exceptions) an innately human capability, one that occurs without any need for formal language instruction. Thus, we are able to acquire language by being immersed in a given culture—regardless of what language or languages are spoken in that culture. This is called language acquisition. There seems to be a language-acquisition window between the ages of 2 and 7 in most human beings when the brain is most open to creating neurological connections that will foster linguistic competence. And although we do not, for example, think in English or any other language (which would mean that language is the prerequisite for thought), there is little doubt that language is not outside of us, like a tool, waiting to be used, but an integral part of who we are, all the time.

More important to understanding the use of language in cultural activities is the idea that, as anthropologist Daniel Nettle puts it, "far from using language simply to communicate information in an optimally efficient way, people use it to create and maintain social identity and social boundaries."[44] Nettle identifies the fact that, theories of language acquisition notwithstanding, language use and cultural identity are linked in some fascinating ways. For example, many linguists have observed that groups will choose to allow or exclude outsiders by the ways in which the groups' members use dialect or specialized vocabularies. In this way they establish the social groups' parameters— and thereby create cultural boundaries. Again, Nettle highlights the point that "There is no necessary correspondence between linguistic boundaries and geographical or physical boundaries.

On the contrary, it is the way language is deployed which creates the social boundaries."[45]

Modern linguistics makes a general distinction between the acts of speech (language performance) and the deep structural grammars at the heart of any language—structures that we internalize by cultural interaction, regardless of our ability to name the rule that governs the performance. English provides a ready example for seeing the distinction between language performance—everyday acts of speaking and writing—and the forms of a given language that instill order on what would otherwise be chaotic (and uncommunicative) acts of performance. The English sentence, "Man bites dog," is different in meaning from a similar syntactic construction, "Dog bites man." The word order (subject, verb, object) structures the meaning. However, the Latin for "man bites dog" could be written *mordet canem* ("he bites the dog") or *canem mordet*. The word order doesn't matter, because the "-*em*" ending of *canem* marks that word as the direct object of a transitive verb.

The virtual community—those separated by distance, but connected by Internet, television, and movies—read, hear, and see acts of speech (performance) that privilege a structural linguistic logic often alien to the languages/cultures where they are consumed. The result is, in one sense, the spread of a version of world culture that flows predominantly from America and the West in general to all "connected" parts of the world. This is one sense of globalization's impact on culture: the spread and influence of language and the cultural effects of its use. But what is the relation of language to culture itself? Is the spread of business English, for example, really a threat to other world cultures that have very different linguistic-cultural foundations? Although there is no definite answer to either of these questions—as is often the case with any topic that involves so many disciplines—an investigation of the idea that different languages spawn different cultures (and that culture influences language evolution) is certainly possible.

The Whorfian Hypothesis

The Whorfian hypothesis (also referred to as the Sapir-Whorf hypothesis or theory) suggests that the language you speak structures the ways that you experience the world and interact with it—and the people in it, of course. An introductory textbook on cultural anthropology explains Whorfian hypothesis as follows:

> The Whorfian hypothesis states that there is a close relationship between the way in which members of a culture perceive their world and the way in which they use their language to communicate their perceptions (their world view). While there seems little doubt that a relationship exists between the categories of a language and those of a culture, Benjamin Lee Whorf went further than most other scholars of his day. He argues that speakers of different languages experience and perceive different realities *because* of the categories of their language. . . . Most anthropologists today would agree with what we can term a weak version of the Whorfian hypothesis, namely, that languages do express cultural emphases and nuances, but that the relationship goes both ways rather than being of the causal form "language structures cultural reality." [46]

We are using this rather extreme view of the relationship between language and culture as a way of getting at the idea of a language/culture/action interface. Most anthropologists would accept a weak version of this hypothesis, though not the extremity of a direct cause-and-effect relationship. It is worth stressing that most linguists would disagree with most anthropologists on this point—as we shall see when we discuss the Great Eskimo Vocabulary Hoax. Whorf published his work on linguistic and cultural connections beginning in the 1930s, but he was indebted to many previous thinkers, including the 19th-century thinker Wilhelm von Humboldt.

Caveat Lector! (Let the Reader Beware!):

The Great Eskimo Vocabulary Hoax

We have been discussing the idea of linguistic relativism and its assumption that "language pervades thought, with different languages causing their speakers to construe reality in different ways."[47] This is a useful way of stressing—especially to Americans raised in one language, English—that those in a language system are unable to recognize that they are *in* a system. Globalization's cultural presence and the ubiquity of American English around the world means that our analogy—language as

The Founder of Linguistic Relativism

One genius within the "age of geniuses" in 19th-century Europe was Wilhelm von Humboldt. "Wilhelm wrote on aesthetics, politics, anthropology, and classical civilization, composed and translated poetry, served as Prussian ambassador to Rome, and founded the University of Berlin that now bears his name and that established the model for university education to the present day. Of course, every age has its universal intellects. But Wilhelm von Humboldt's greatest passion was distinctive for his age, for he made himself into the founder of modern linguistic study. Linguists from the later 18th century had been discovering the seemingly universal relationships of human languages and hence of human cultures. Goethe (who read at least seven languages and explored the literatures of many others) coined the term *world literature*; Friedrich Schlegel (poet, literary critic, philosopher, historian of culture, theologian) studied Sanskrit, the oldest relic of the Indo-European language family, and wrote an influential book on the language and wisdom of the Indians. . . . But Humboldt's striving for universality outdid them all. He went into unrelated territory, learning well over a hundred languages including the most exotic that could be investigated—Basque, American Indian languages, and the Kavi language of what is now Indonesia. . . . For Humboldt, as for many others . . . social difference was crucial, and above all the difference among societies that arise from linguistic difference. Humboldt famously referred to language as a 'world within the world': the language that you speak governs all of your perceptions."*

* Quoted in *The Longman Anthology of World Literature Volume E: The Nineteenth Century*, Marshall Brown and Bruce Robbins, eds. New York: Pearson, 2004, p. 5.

a map that is linked to culture, purpose-driven, and therefore an interface with the diversity of many world cultures—is useful. However, the dominant thrust of linguistic theory since the late 1950s, beginning with a brilliant thinker named Noam Chomsky, has been that there is a universal, biological "language instinct" that unites all human peoples. Thus, while our analogy of language as a map is useful as a way of getting at ideas concerned with our interactions with other cultures and subcultures, it is important that we not take it too far or insist that language is an absolute prerequisite for thought in a given language. An example of a pervasive hoax can help to show the other side of the linguistic coin, one that stresses the "deep structures" of language that all humans share and contradicts the notion of linguistic relativism.

Steven Pinker is a former student of Chomsky's and an influential writer on linguistics and our sense of how the mind operates when it uses language—any language. In his bestselling popularization of Chomsky's linguistic theories, entitled *The Language Instinct*, Pinker summarizes an exposé of the widely held notion that Eskimos have more words than other cultures for the word "snow" because the concept has more importance for them than for, say, tropical inhabitants. This popular myth is a result of a half-century of too-ready adherence to a "strong" version of the Sapir-Whorf theory. Speaking of unfounded or false stories, Pinker writes that:

> no discussion of language and thought would be complete without the Great Eskimo Vocabulary Hoax. Contrary to popular belief, the Eskimos do not have more words for snow than do speakers of English. They do not have four hundred words for snow, as it has been claimed in print . . . or even nine. One dictionary puts the number at two. Counting generously, experts can come up with about a dozen, but by such standards English would not be far behind. . . . Where did the myth come from? Not from anyone who has ever actually studied the Yupik and Inuit-Inupiaq families of . . . languages.[48]

Pinker summarizes the commonsensical power of linguistic relativism—and the immense appeal of thinking condescendingly about exotic cultures as immeasurably stranger than our own—as a way of forcing his readers to confront a too-easy attachment to Whorf's hypothesis.

For our purposes, viewing language as a powerful pre-determiner—as a filter or a map of the mind—will suffice. Language use and cultural dissimilarity are linked, though we need not decide, ultimately, whether there is a causal relationship. An example of how language structure is affiliated to cultural action can help clarify the issue.

Do You Call Your Teacher "Sir" or "Ma'am"?

This example concerns what are called "honorifics," terms that convey respect and social status, like "Professor," "Dr.," or "Sir." The speech performance of American English speakers makes no mention of whether the relationship between speaker and listener is formal or informal. However, in German and French (there are many other examples), a speaker uses a formal pronoun or verb form that marks the relationship as such. In French, the pronoun for "you," *vous* (formal) or *tu* (informal) is a strong marker of cultural relations. One does not switch from the required *vous* form until asked to do so; the *tu* form is generally reserved for family and intimate friends. In German, the verb forms for polite and familiar forms are themselves different. For example, to ask "Are you going?" one would say *Gehen sie?* in the formal register (the one that should always be used in public space), and *Gehst du?* if allowed to enter the familiar zone. In fact, there is a rather charming ritual in German that invites a speaker into the informal zone. In America, we are often told, "Just call me Bob." This same event would happen in German ("Just call me Hans," for example), but German pronouns—unlike their English counterparts—can be formal or informal. Even after being told to "Call me Hans," a bilingual English-German student from America in

Berlin, for example, would be well advised to use the formal pronoun when referring to Hans until Hans told him something like "*Du kahnst mich duzen*"—you are now a part of my informal zone, in essence.

English has no such linguistic markers in the language itself. The appropriateness of address is culturally determined by context—a presupposition that can create some embarrassing interactions when speakers ignore nuanced contexts and the variability of social and cultural expectations. Other language structures, ancient Japanese and Egyptian, for example, have strict markers for word usage that differentiate between a large number of social groups and castes. In these cases, language use is firmly connected to social class.

To return to the example of word order creating syntactic meaning (the "man bites dog" example), we can see that cultural behavior can be a result of linguistic structures. Americans often interrupt each other when speaking together. This is not always just rudeness, since a claim can be made that by seeing where the sentence is going—because word order matters— and "finishing the other person's thought," we are creating a common bond by affirming our understanding when we attempt to infer the finishing words that will complete the thought. Listen to your peers speak. You will hear a lot of "It's like, . . . you know?" These fillers in speech are also signaling a form of interpersonal connection—a cultural bond created by language—because, "It's like, well . . . you *know*!" We very often *do* know, and that's the point: common cultural and linguistic foundations allow for interruptions and gaps that we in America "understand" as normal. Certain cultural contexts—in business, academia, and elsewhere—treat interruptions as rude regardless of implied linguistic assumptions, because the structure of power relationships implies that authority gets to speak without interruption. Those who have not been acculturated to this sort of cultural code-switching will not get contracts, better grades, or respect unless they mimic the external language they experience in these differing American contexts.

In German, however, interruptions are linguistically foolish: how can you possibly know where the sentence is "going" if the main verb can appear at the very end of the sentence? Obviously, Germans can generally foresee what a verb in a given sentence will be, and interruptions do happen. The point of the example is to stress the fact that other cultures' languages operate differently than American English does, and to establish how cultural activity can flow from those differences. While there is no need to assume a cause-and-effect relationship between each linguistic-cultural apparatus (English versus German) and the relative degree of informality that marks each culture (public discourse in German happens to be much more formal than it is in America), the marked degree of informality in cultural space in America can be seen clearly through the lens of linguistic structure.

LANGUAGE AND POWER

None of us really needs to be reminded that those who control access to language also control access to power within a given culture. At one time, for example, children were expected to be "seen and not heard." Those who get to "speak" occupy a privileged space within kinship and other cultural groups. Further, privileging one type of speech (or dialect) within a given language creates a hierarchy of socially acceptable patterns of usage. When Latin was the official, administrative language of Europe—from about 300 B.C. until the 18th century or so—the languages of the various cultural groups that the Roman Empire controlled were subordinated. Those cultures were, therefore, also subordinated by virtue of the fact that all business and political activities were conducted in Latin alone. In order to participate in even mundane matters, local groups needed to be able to participate in and access Latin, regardless of their own, household language or dialect.

Braveheart

The 1995 movie *Braveheart*, which starred Mel Gibson, can help illustrate the subordinate status of linguistic groups who are not in control of the dominant language. The movie is about the emergence of a Scottish national hero, William Wallace, and his attempts to help his people to overthrow the oppressive yoke of England—personified in the character of King Edward I (Longshanks). The French-born wife of the king's son has been sent to distract Wallace as the king prepares to crush the Scottish rebellion. Wallace, the queen, and one of the king's counselors are in a tent, beginning to discuss the situation. Unsurprisingly, they are speaking in English (modern English, for the purposes of the film), though the queen is multilingual, having been acculturated in the French language and trained in Latin, the language of diplomacy and power. The king's counselor becomes disturbed by Wallace's confrontational tone and switches from English to Latin, calling Wallace a "barbarian." Wallace shocks both queen and counselor by responding in Latin and then speaks to the queen in French. The idea that a barbarian, dressed in a kilt, dirty from hard living in the mountains of the Scottish Highlands, can speak Latin, astonishes the queen so much that she sends the counselor from the room and begins to treat this intriguing cultural specimen with real respect.

Latin was the official language of political activity throughout Europe until quite recently. In fact, John Milton—one of the greatest English poets—served as Secretary of Foreign Tongues to the English Council of State under Oliver Cromwell from 1649 until 1652. Milton's job was to negotiate language's barriers, translating documents from English into Latin and vice versa, because all national entities conducted their business in this "master" language. This remnant of the long-defunct Roman Empire held sway due to its status as the official language of the Holy Roman Empire, through which the Catholic Church exercised its dominion over secular rulers.

French was for many years the "official" diplomatic language of the European-influenced world, as we observed when we mentioned the Berlin Congress of 1884–1885. The United Nations' various mottoes appear in French in the building in New York City that houses the "world's voices."

We have already seen that English language instruction (in India and in the United States) has been used for the purposes of cultural control. In present-day America, where 27 states have already passed "English as Official Language" laws, many people intuitively understand the language/culture/power linkage. A book published in 2004 by author Samuel Huntington warns of the spread of Spanish-language culture in the southwestern and southern United States. His thesis, in *Who Are We?: The Challenges to America's National Identity*, is that English-speaking cultural communities will be overwhelmed by the growing number of Spanish-only cultural communities, as Mexicans and other Hispanic groups attemp to retain their cultural identities in multicultural America.

The United States Congress has already attempted to pass legislation that would recognize English as the official language of the federal government. On August 1, 1995, The House of Representatives passed H.R. Bill 123, *The English Language Empowerment Act.* The bill would, in the words of its sponsor, "require that all official government business be conducted in English and would repeal a federal law mandating that states with large concentrations of non-English-speaking voters provide bilingual voting ballots. . . . The purpose of H.R. 123 is to . . . bind us together through the use of English as our common language . . .[empowering] individuals to become successful members of our society . . .[empowering] each new generation of immigrants with access to the American dream." [49]

Even as America struggles with the issue of language and cultural power within its own borders, much of the rest of the world is faced with the influential power of English and its cultural attachments as a globalizing phenomenon.

ENGLISH AS *LINGUA FRANCA*

Much has been written about the fear that international English usage will obliterate native languages. The concern is tied to globalization's English-language business face. In Chapter 7, we will examine the transmission of global culture in English, very often in American English. Mark Twain famously remarked that England and America are "two countries separated by a common language." British-English usage is not in all ways the same as American English (or with Australian English or Canadian English either, for that matter). Without pretending that they are the same, however, we can speak of "English" generally as some form of the language most of us speak in America, especially that which is used in business or in American popular culture. The next chapter will examine some of these issues, especially as they relate to the culture-specific baggage that is often assumed in language rather than overtly stated. For example, idiomatic usage (cliches, etc.) are notoriously difficult for non-native speakers. When a South African graduate student at Columbia University was warned by his advisor that he was "way out in left field" when he submitted an essay, the student— fluent in English, but not embedded in American culture— interpreted the criticism of his opinion as a positive: After all, this meant that he was "in the game." Some experts have estimated that 80 percent of the world's computer code is written in English, and English is the commonly accepted language of international business. Indians in Mumbai (Bombay) take not only English classes, but also American-dialect English classes as training for the growing number of customer-service jobs that support American and international conglomerates. The fear that international English usage will obliterate native languages is, generally, misplaced, although the strength of American popular culture's transmission is almost immeasurably powerful.

The Transmission of the Modernist Dream: Ideological and Cultural Transfers

Globalization is not an American phenomenon, though much of its cultural face involves American icons and cultural trends. Globalization is also not about the worldwide spread of the idea of the "American Dream," but some common elements of this cultural myth are bound up in a general sense of the globalizing movement—scientifically rational, economically efficient, based upon individualism, ultimately democratic and transnational (Figure 7.1). The American dream of individual success, of living "better" than your parents, is a subset of what we call the modernist dream, or modernism. The worldwide spread of Starbucks, the coffeehouse chain, illustrates both the fears of antiglobalization activists and the dangers of presuming that culture—even that of a super-culture like America—flows in only one direction.

Figure 7.1 On June 5, 1989, this lone man, on his way back from the grocery with bags in his hands, faced off with a line of tanks in Tiananmen Square, Beijing. The Chinese government crushed this student-led demonstration for democratic reform and killed many in the clash. This man was pulled away by bystanders and the tanks continued on their way.

This chapter will focus on the power and possibilities of globalization's cultural aspects, even as it allows for a more nuanced understanding of the difficulties involved in creating a unified, worldwide culture.

HORATIO ALGER AND THE AMERICAN DREAM

Work hard and your individual actions will be rewarded, because opportunities for success are available to all. That, in a nutshell, is the myth of the American Dream, whose elements

The Case of a Cup of Coffee

One of the many, sometimes unacknowledged, contributions of Islamic culture over the past thousand years is the introduction of coffee drinking into Europe in the 17th century. Africans on the fertile slopes of the Ethiopian highlands had chewed coffee beans for energy long before introducing the bean to Arabic traders on the coast. The tremendous popularity of brewed coffee eventually made one port, Al-Makkha (from which we get the word *mocha*), prosperous and famous from India to Egypt.

A military battle led to the introduction of coffee into Europe and the eventual growth (especially in Vienna and Zurich) of café culture. In 1683, the Austrians, Germans, and Poles routed the Ottoman Turks from a prolonged siege of Vienna. The legend has it that 500 bags of coffee beans were left behind by the retreating Turks, leading to the soon-widespread drinking of coffee in cafés throughout first Vienna and eventually the world.

When Starbucks opened its first coffee shop in Zurich in 2003, critics of globalization "railed against the 'homogenization' of global culture and the threat of 'monoculture'—that is, the worldwide replacement of individual, indigenous stores and restaurants with international chains."* The Seattle-based chain of franchises has taken its style, according to writer Jackson Kuhl, from Italian coffee houses that were descendents of the Viennese models. Kuhl cites a Starbuck's executive admitting that the chain used "Italian-sounding nonsense language" (like "frappucino" and "Tazo tea") as a way of making its brand more exotic-sounding. In a nice turn of phrase, Kuhl concludes that "Starbuck's customers, whether in Zurich or Beirut, are drinking an American version of an Italian evolution of a beverage invented by Arabs brewed from a bean discovered by Africans."**

* Adapted from Jackson Kuhl, "Tempest in a Teapot: Starbucks Invades the World," *Reason* vol. 34 (January 2003): 56.
** Ibid., p. 57.

include the ownership of a private home in a safe neighbor-hood, affordable healthcare and education, material comfort in the form of possessions (called **commodity culture**), and with a rewarding career. The promise of the free-enterprise system combined with the dismantling of barriers to free trade (where no one country charges tariffs, or taxes on imported goods, in an attempt to protect national markets) have created an inter-national version of this national myth. It is a myth not because it is false, but because, like all myths, it is a story that "explains" how large, poorly understood forces operate. Perhaps the most famous promulgator of the myth of the American Dream was the 19th-century writer Horatio Alger. According to the official Horatio Alger website, these books helped "to encourage the spirit of Strive and Succeed that for half of a century guided Alger's undaunted heroes—lads whose struggles epitomized the great American dream and inspired hero ideals in countless millions of young Americans."[50] The titles of just a few of his books give an indication of the morals of his stories: *Joe the Hotel Boy, Or Winning Out by Pluck*; *The Errand Boy: Or How Phil Brent Won Success*; *Paul the Peddler: Or the Fortunes of a Young Street Merchant*. His books spun endless variations on the same plot: a young boy, often a homeless orphan, seizes an opportunity to improve his lot in life by working hard, regardless of the obstacles and lack of immediate success. His reward is a secure place in the economic hierarchy. The moral is worth repeating, because it lies at the heart of why you are today in school: perseverance and individual effort will be rewarded. Today, education operates as a launching pad—presumably an equally available one, though that is debatable—for opportunity. (We explored the linkage to language usage as an integral com-ponent in success in Chapter 6.)

Although Alger's boy-heroes are the stuff of the past, and were even parodied during his lifetime, the power of the American Dream that his stories present is still very much alive. The American notion of opportunity lives on. To underline the point that opportunity is connected to education, and is available to all in a free society as long as you work for it, the motto of the Horatio Alger Association for Distinguished Americans states:

> The Association brings the "Horatio Alger Heroes" of today together with those of tomorrow by bestowing the Horatio Alger Award each year and by awarding more than $5 million annually in college scholarships to young people. Horatio Alger Scholars have faced challenges and realize that a college education is the avenue to a better future.[51]

The American Dream as a Subset of Cultural Modernity

Access to opportunity, upward social mobility, and the promise of success through individual activity are the watchwords of modernism in general. **Modernism** is a term that refers to the tradition of European rational inquiry, which includes the scientific method of empirical proof rather than unsubstantiated (usually religious) belief. Another way of putting it is that there is a "homogenizing worldwide process of modernization [that] has become irreversible. All human communities are gradually but inexorably coming to resemble each other, exhibiting the same, salient characteristics of a modern society."[52] The "civilizing mission" that was one justification of British control over its colonies is one outgrowth of this tradition, which began in roughly 1600 and continues, with some important permutations, to this day. As we discussed in Chapter 4, one of the hallmarks of imperialism in general was the ideology that human progress worldwide could be compared to individual human development. Thus, some cultures were "mature," and others were still "childlike." There is a cultural myth at the heart of this concept as well: that of a civilization's progress towards some presumed goal. That goal is the rational, modern state, with its models of so-called democratic rule (of various sorts) and the triumph of the individual. The story of history according to this myth is that of a step-by-step movement in every culture toward the presumable perfection of modern (European- and American-style) culture. It is very important to realize that this is an ideology, not a fact. Historical development is not goal-oriented towards some final utopian civilization. Changes in cultural and social structures are not uniform and predestined. Rather, cultural changes are the result of random sociopolitical and other forces.

Postmodernism's Challenge to Modernism

The concept of postmodernism is the ideology, say many scholars, that explains our present state of belief in much of the industrialized world. Modernism is characterized by a belief in "wholeness": the world is coherent, ordered, and knowable. If reason is applied to the conditions of the world with enough intensity over enough time, all the aspects of the world can be understood. A physical map, as discussed in Chapter 5, is an analogy for modernism. Once all the indistinct areas on a map of the world are filled in by exploration, the map is complete. Modernism assumes that objective knowledge of the world is possible. **Postmodernism**, on the other hand, insists that knowledge is not objectively "out there" waiting to be discovered, but rather that each of us creates a subjective version of reality based upon ideological beliefs and individual cultural experiences. Postmodernism rejects the notion of the map (modernism) in favor of the analogy of the collage; fragmentation, not unity, is the reality of knowledge. A collage is composed of any number of not necessarily related pictures, items, or texts: each viewer of a collage constructs his or her own meaning of the relationships of the items that are juxtaposed. There is no total "meaning." One can never really know all there is to know about anything, but understands fragments of knowledge that are bound up in one's subjective position in the world. This sounds complex, and it is. The relationship between globalization and culture is in the final analysis equally complex.

Postmodernists take comfort in this complexity. Rather than fretting about an inability to understand it all—whether the "it" at hand is globalization or any other form of totalizing theory of how the world works—postmodernists embrace the notion that fragmentary understanding is the only understanding that is ever possible. Skepticism about the ultimate ability to understand dynamic movements through the exercise of reason is a hallmark of postmodernism. The thinking that characterizes an "either this or that" kind of thinking is linked to modernism; there must be either this way or that way of thinking about the world. Postmodernism suggests that "either-or" thinking is an attempt to understand wholeness; it seeks a "both this and that" understanding, even as it acknowledges the fragmentary, incoherent nature of reality as a whole. Postmodernism has developed as a different way of understanding the world, and some find relief in its acceptance of subtlety and nuance rather than total understanding.

THE END OF THE COLD WAR

Thomas Friedman and other analysts of globalization speak of a "paradigm shift" at the end of the Cold War, when the United States and the Soviet Union faced off for control of the world. A paradigm is a set of beliefs that defines the ways in which we think and act, a way of viewing the world. A paradigm shift occurs when society sees the world through a new mindset. Every element of international relationships under this Cold War paradigm was seen through the filter of superpower relationships. The Cold War paradigm was a binary opposition: a two-sided view of the world. In this case, the democratic, capitalist West was opposed by socialist and communist nation–states such as the U.S.S.R. and the People's Republic of China. The "new" paradigm is much more fragmented: new nation–states are emerging, ethnic and religious conflicts are multiplying. The "world" is no longer profitably viewed through a binary lens. The fall of the Berlin Wall in late 1989 was a

Figure 7.2 A resident of West Berlin swings a sledgehammer, trying to destroy the Berlin Wall near Potsdamer Platz on November 12, 1989.

physical marker of a paradigm shift (Figure 7.2). Such shifts do not occur on a given day, but are cultural movements that ebb and flow over long periods until the new paradigm takes complete hold; we have used historical events throughout this text as markers simply as a way of landing on signal issues.

(An excellent example of a paradigm shift can be seen in the growing cultural awareness of 17th-century Europe that the earth was not the center of the solar system.)

Friedman puts it well: "globalization has replaced the Cold War as the defining international system." But what does this mean? He continues, writing, "as an international system, the Cold War had its own structure of power: the balance between the United States and the U.S.S.R. The Cold War had its own rules . . . and perspectives on the world,"[53] which were characterized by a simplistic, two-sided division. As we have already observed, also via Friedman, the "globalization system . . . has one overarching feature—integration."[54] The standard explanation for the disintegration of the Soviet empire has to do with economic policy, but there are some who believe that the West's spread of cultural images and ideologies created a subcurrent of popular dissatisfaction within the Soviet Union that made its continued isolation from the world (except on its own terms) untenable. At the present time, only North Korea is entirely "off the grid" of the Internet, its citizens unable to access the World Wide Web: a recognition by this totalitarian regime's leaders that Western cultural artifacts and ideologies that present a different ideology than the one practiced in North Korea would "infect" its people.

CELEBRITY CULTURE

Celebrity culture and its spread is one arena of interest relative to globalization. English soccer star David Beckham (who now plays for the soccer team Real Madrid) and his equally famous wife, Victoria Beckham (the former Posh Spice of the pop band Spice Girls) are almost unable to appear in public in much of Asia for fear of being mobbed by fans. As a mark of celebrity culture's power, it in interesting to note that in 1998 Beckham was the first Western celebrity to appear on an advertising billboard in Iran since the rise of a fundamentalist Iranian state in 1979.

The Indian film industry (dubbed "Bollywood") is one of a number of "regional" producers of mass culture whose icons have an effect in many other parts of the globe. Although many pop culture stars and products have purely limited, regional influence, many others project an image far beyond local, cultural markets. The mass movements of people (through migration, exile, or exodus) carry culture along with them. For example, the very large Pakistani population in London has created a thriving economic culture based upon "take-away," that is, take-out Indian food. Of course, international television (like the British Broadcasting Company's World Service and the seemingly ubiquitous MTV) spreads style, music, and images of all sorts to far-flung places.

In Nigeria, a large nation–state in western Africa, it is not at all unusual—even in farming villages far from major cities like Lagos—to see television antennas on homes that serve as cultural hubs for the extended family unit that is the norm in much of sub-Saharan Africa. (Any blood relation is considered "immediate family," eligible for any help and access the clan can provide.) MTV-style images of Western consumer culture drift into cultures without a frame of reference fit to examine the sometimes-outlandish behavior of the actors. This becomes, by representation, "America." Imagine yourself building an understanding of the United States based solely upon T.V. shows like *Baywatch* or teen-angst dramas like *Party of Five* (the latter an American show that was a staple of Chinese television in the late 1990s). Issues of body image, appropriate inter-gender behaviors, and of course the ideology behind commodity culture (buy more, now) transfer themselves in waves as such images become the "face" of the modern world for developing countries. As we have already observed, people are not puppets, but the influence of images from America and the West influence, for example, behaviors, styles, and other cultural activities in many other parts of the world.

The Strange Case of David Hasselhoff

We all know that celebrities—the stars of movies, sports, television, and music—wield astonishing influence in media of all sorts in America and elsewhere. As satellite technology becomes more readily available around the world, it will become increasingly difficult for countries to control what their people see on their televisions. Even before satellite dishes and the Internet, worldwide distribution of television shows, movies, music, and fashion, transmitted by regional, sometimes national media outlets created virtual communities around the world that shared images and culture created far from their local environments. In many cases, celebrities see themselves as cultural magnets—creating trends, embodying ideological clarity, and "managing" (in their persons) the forces that are dispersed throughout cultural groups. Witness political speeches by movie stars or the popularization of previously little-known theories by celebrities.

An example of this last might be seen in Madonna's "franchising" of Kabbalah shops. Kabbalah is an ancient and esoteric strand of the Jewish religion based on a mystical interpretation of the Bible. There are now "shops" that "sell" this icon's spiritual understanding, such as it is. Madonna's various reincarnations of her celebrity persona now include the marketing of a spiritual activity. In the extreme case that follows, a figure from celebrity culture has taken responsibility for the spread of democratic ideologies.

David Hasselhoff and the Fall of the Berlin Wall

A useful example of the self-delusion—but undeniable power—of celebrity culture can be found in David Hasselhoff's claim that he has been overlooked as an engine of change in the fall of the Berlin Wall and the ideological reunification of the German people of West and East Germany. Speaking in 2003 to "German TV's *Spielfilm* magazine, the 51-year-old carped about how his

pivotal role in harmonizing relations between the two
sides had been overlooked. . . . 'I find it a bit sad that there
is no photo of me hanging on the walls in the Berlin
Museum at Checkpoint Charlie.'"[55]

The California-based television show *Baywatch* has had
an extremely wide syndication around the world. Its life-
guard star, David Hasselhoff, was also the leading actor in
another show that appeared in many world markets,
especially in Europe. That show, *Knight Rider*, with its
technologically advanced "talking" car, was shown in a
great number of world markets even after it had disap-
peared from American television. For those who know
him primarily as an American television actor, it may be
surprising to learn that Hasselhoff has had an immense
influence on German cultural activity (Figure 7.3).
Hasselhoff had become a pop-singing star in Germany,
Austria, and Switzerland in the late 1980s, when he
decided to remake a German pop song that had been a
hit almost 20 years earlier. In 1989, Hasselhoff released
an English-language version of that song, originally titled
Auf Der Strasse Nach Suden. His version, "I've Been
Looking for Freedom," became a smash hit. As West
Germans clamored for reunification with East Germany,
and the Berlin Wall itself came under attack by students,
Hasselhoff's sentimental ballad became an unofficial
anthem for protesters. Its lyrics included much that could
be easily adapted to the situation: "I've been lookin' for
freedom; I've been lookin' so long; I've been lookin' for
freedom; still the search goes on."[56]

It is very easy to make fun of a person's claim—usually based
only on personal popularity—that he or she is "important"
in political, or spiritual, or economic spheres by virtue of
popularity alone. Authority in one field (entertainment or
sports, for example) does not transfer automatically to other

Figure 7.3 David Hasselhoff found an enthusiastic audience in Germany. In January 31, 2004, he presented his new album, "David Sings America" during a television show in Magdeburg, eastern Germany.

fields. Logicians call this the fallacy of false authority. However, amusement aside, Hasselhoff's situation allows us to pay attention to the very real, very powerful role that some individuals serve in the larger field of globalizing culture: these individuals become icons, people who embody a set of cultural practices and ideological beliefs that can then be transmitted across cultural boundaries, "wrapped" in the persona of the celebrity. Thus, celebrity culture carries with it modernist cultural values.

Even individuals who would respect modernism's values—especially the principle that rational rather than spiritual activity is the hallmark of human activity—can and do affect immense cultural currents, especially because communications technologies can spread the word so quickly. For example, Pope

John Paul II was widely credited—even by former Soviet Premier Mikhail Gorbachev—with the fall of the Berlin Wall as the now-deceased Catholic pontiff had supported workers' rights movements in Poland, East Germany, and elsewhere. Individuals do affect culture.

The Movement
of Goods and People

Among the most powerful claims made by advocates of tariff-free global trade is that globalization leads to an increased awareness of universal human rights in non-democratic cultures. In the words of a fictional character on the American television show *The West Wing*, "at least we hope so . . . nothing else has worked." The growth of Western-style franchising (of fast-food, of theme parks, of service operations) in developing parts of the world provides an introduction to market capitalism in the form of jobs that allows for individual self-determination. Further, such jobs create a middle class with disposable incomes that can be spent on those elements of commodity culture described in Chapter 7. For example, the dramatic increase in jobs previously done in home markets (generally referred to in America as the "outsourcing" of jobs) by people in India has led to the rise of a commodity-conscious culture, especially among Indian women in India's major cities. Readers are advised to consult the Further Reading list at the end of the book. They will see that many scholars are looking at this and other issues related to the interrelationship of globalization and culture in a variety of ways.

This brief chapter will not pretend to be an exhaustive treatment of the crucial issue of human rights; rather, it will focus on one specific cultural activity in Zambia, called *salaula*, that can serve as a thinking exercise on the topic and show a transition from the cultural power carried by goods to a brief sketch of one type of cultural power related to the movement of people.

GOVERNMENTAL ATTEMPTS AT CHARITABLE GIVING AND CULTURAL INFLUENCE

That those who have much should give to those who have little is a doctrine rooted in many religious ideologies. Islam reminds its believers that giving to the poor is a requirement; the Judeo-Christian tradition stresses the need to care for those in need; Hinduism, with its belief in reincarnation, allows its followers to see themselves in others less-well-off because, in the next life, that lot might indeed be theirs.

Even one of the justifications for British colonial activity in India is related to the idea of charity. The British used the ideology of the "civilizing mission"—enlightened, Christian ideas brought to the heathen pagan—as a foundation for its existence in India. The first stanza of Rudyard Kipling's famous poem, "The White Man's Burden" (1899) sums up the projection of noblesse oblige (the obligation of the nobility) that lies at this justification's core:

> Take up the White Man's burden—
> Send forth the best ye breed—
> Go bind your sons to exile
> To serve your captives' need;
> To wait in heavy harness,

> On fluttered folk and wild—
> Your new-caught, sullen peoples,
> Half-devil and half-child.

The poem was addressed to the American people as their country assumed control of the Philippines at the end of the Spanish-American War. More generally, Americans were challenged to go forth as the English had ("send forth the best ye breed") and serve their imperial empires by helping subject people (who were part children, part devils) to come into the "mature" fullness of a civilization perceived as evolutionary by affiliating with the West (which would acculturate the "sullen peoples").

More recently, governments practice charity that is called, in America, foreign aid. It seems self-evidently "right" that rich societies should share their wealth with developing countries. Altruism—an absence of self-interest—is not necessarily the root of such international beneficence, however, any more than it was the root of imperialism. Nation–states have a stake in promoting positive images throughout regions of the world where people struggle for daily existence. Whatever the motivation, governments give direct aid to other nation–states, and they participate in extragovernmental activities such as the United Nations to create international harmony.

According to economist Paolo Paiscolon, however, "most recipients of U.S. development aid are poorer now than they were before first receiving it. From 1980 to 2000, the U.S. disbursed 167 billion dollars to 156 developing countries. Among the 97 countries that have reliable economic data covering that period, median per capita gross domestic product declined from $1,076 in 1980 to $994 in 2000."[57] In other words, without factoring in the reality of inflation, which lowers the purchasing power of dollars over time, an average Zambian, for example, saw a decrease in his yearly income, even after substantial charitable governmental aid. The colossal failure of this massive giving, according to Paiscolon, is in large part due to the vague conditions attached to the aid, the corruption of many Third-World nations, and the failure of the aid to find its way to those most in need.

Beginning on March 1, 2004, the American government began a program called the Millennium Challenge Account (MCA). This initiative is part of a long-term attempt to increase American foreign aid by 50 percent, but it is linking the aid to "people-based," not just infrastructural, construction projects. Such construction projects will continue to be funded, but the administration will require that those nation–states that receive these grants (funds that do not need to be repaid) must embrace MCA's goals of good governance, including audited reviews of expenditures to negate the corrosive effects of corruption; a commitment to universal human rights, especially for women and children; a commitment to providing increased health and educational access for all the people in the nation–state that accepts a grant; and the adoption of policies to foster free enterprise and entrepreneurship.[58] This program mirrors others that have attempted to provide small grants-in-aid to women entrepreneurs in Africa and elsewhere. The direct linkage between charity and the development of a modernist, Western-style focus on human rights and the development of individual embrace of free-market capitalism is apparent.

On a more personal level, many Americans give to international aid efforts that are solicited on television and through the mail and the Internet. The grim pictures of dying children and starving people in war- and disease-ridden regions of the world are undeniably affecting. It takes a charitable organization with great depth and expertise to deliver such aid to where it needs to go, however, and some have criticized the large percentage of charitable dollars that go to administrative overhead rather than to the relief of human suffering. Even in a smaller sense, though, our charity can have an effect in the global arena, as the practice of *salaula* (described in the following section) shows.

Last, it is difficult to separate true charity from public perceptions that hidden motives are at the root of the reason that developed countries give to the poor, needy, and struggling people of the Third World. For example, there is no denying the good that many Christian missionaries do in their service throughout the world, but the history of colonialism makes plain that the "civilizing mission"—even when entirely well intentioned—can be problematic. The worldwide outpouring of financial and logistical support for those most affected by the cataclysmic tsunami of late 2004 meant that many in the developed world—especially in dominantly Christian countries like the United States—offered support during a time of crisis. However, some commentators—in America, Europe, and the Arab world—tried to estimate the amount of "good press" that the United States (in particular) might have counted upon by giving to the aid effort. Because of the ongoing Iraqi conflict's polarization of Muslim sentiment about America, some commentators suggested that America was driven less by altruism and more by attempts to generate positive feelings in, especially, Indonesia—the largest Muslim country on the planet. Perceptions often trump reality.

It is not cynical to think beyond the surface, and charitable giving is a particularly complex issue for those who give as well as those who receive. A case in point can be found in the country of Zambia in Africa.

Salaula

Many people in America, when cleaning out their closets, take their used clothing to charitable organizations such the St. Vincent de Paul Society or The Salvation Army. Some such organizations typically run discounted clothing stores, where the sales support their charitable efforts. However, have you ever considered that the amount given cannot possibly be held in the little shops that sell such cast-offs? In the United Kingdom, for example, "about one million tons of old clothes" are thrown away each year and "an estimated 200,000 tons are recycled to be worn again or used in industry."[59] There is also, however, a thriving international market in used clothing in which donated clothing is sold to exporters for resale in developing countries. The tee shirt you discarded last year might well be on the back of an African youngster, advertising your high-school football team to a culture for whom "football" equals soccer.

Michael Durham, a reporter for the British newspaper, *The Guardian*, followed the trail of a particular blouse, "a cheerful, summery thing," from its home as a cast-off in a small community in England, placed with good intentions in a bin outside a supermarket, to its eventual home in a used-clothing market in Zambia. Zambia is a poor country in south central Africa. It had been a colony of the United Kingdom called Northern Rhodesia until its independence in 1964. It has long been a recipient of foreign aid of all sorts, but its inhabitants are among the poorest in the world.

Durham notes, "By dropping the blouse into the charity bank, [the donor] ensures that a small portion of its value will benefit Scope, the organization for people with cerebral palsy."[60] The donor has a moment of good feeling about her donation, but her sense that she has "given something" to the poor is a bit misplaced. A large company, Ragtex UK, will collect the blouse as a part of the 95 tons of old clothing it collects each week from just this one part of England. The managing director of Ragtex estimates that "Only about 10–20 percent of the clothes collected in charity shops are sold in Britain to be worn in Britain. . . .We sort and grade the clothes, package them up and sell them abroad in countries where they are really needed, like Pakistan and southern Africa."[61] Similar operations function in the United States.

The clothing is bundled into huge bales that weigh about 200 pounds apiece and transported to Zambia. At warehouses in the capital city of Lusaka, hundreds of Zambians—including many women—line up to buy a bundle apiece in the import warehouse. These individual bundles become the capital investment that can be pieced into individual sales in market stalls many hours and miles away from the capital city. Open-air markets are filled with entrepreneurs selling their goods, used clothing from the West, hoping to recover their capital outlay and begin again. Durham describes the "thousands of market stalls [throughout Africa] overflowing with secondhand western clothing, Gap T-shirts, Levi Jeans, Nike trainers, Marks & Spencer cargo pants. ...At times it seems the whole of Africa seems to be an immense open-air bazaar of western hand-me-downs."[62]

Zambians call the old clothing business *salaula*–a word signifying "to rummage in a pile. And that is what millions of Zambians do daily, to keep looking spruce."[63] Appearing well-kempt, even in used clothing, is important in Zambian society. And although foreign nationals working in Zambia find that "constant handouts demean the individual... [so] it is better to sell the clothes than give them away," not everyone agrees that wearing salaula clothing "stands for opportunity, choice and new chances."[64] "Many Zambians... believe salaula is western relief aid that has somehow been hijacked and sold for a profit, on the basis of the British and American charity price tags that are still attached to [some of] the clothes."[65]

While salaula appears to be a model of entrepreneurial development, there are other sides to this story. For example, the popularity of the salaula market has been blamed for the collapse of the Zambian textile industry: "in the seven years before 1993, no fewer than 51 out of 72 Zambian clothing firms closed down."[66] There is no denying, though, that entrepreneurial activity in businesses unthought-of in the West have cultural effects, and can, potentially, lead to increased possibilities for people—especially women—otherwise frozen out of access to business opportunities.

THE UNCONSIDERED ISSUE OF WOMEN
Western images of "free" women viewed in cultures that consider women less-than-equal have had an undeniable effect.

In some Arabic countries, women are not even allowed to go out in public, let alone drive a car. The culture of that home country may experience internal problems if large numbers of marginalized populations get to see that there are other ways of living. Such a process is tied to the ways in which images become internalized by those who see them. Many cultures reject what they see as the sordid, decadent nature of Western-style advertising and media imagery, so a slow, partial movement seems more likely than not. Some Arabic women are agitating for increased freedom within their cultures, and many of these women cite Western modes of human rights as the basis for their claims (Figure 8.1).

In Turkey, for example, a series of events has occurred that illustrates the intersection of culture/politics/economics. The Turkish government is very interested in joining the European Union (EU), but has to date been unsuccessful. Among the many ostensible reasons for the EU's reluctance to admit Turkey include the charge that Turkey's record of human rights is not up to the European par. An unstated reason might be the 80 million Muslims in Turkey. Membership in the EU allows member citizens to travel relatively freely across national boundaries for work and other reasons. The economic benefits that will flow to Turkey from this sociopolitical alliance will likely have many cultural effects, for Turkey and the member nations of the EU as well. Although we often think only of media when we initially consider globalizing culture, the movement of people is the still the single most powerful cultural force in the world. As people around the world glimpse alternatives to the restrictions inherent in their own cultures (all cultures are by definition restrictive, as they allow and disallow certain practices), some will move from their home cultures. The net effect is a form of cultural affiliation tied to elements of the globalizing movement of modernism. A recent news report ties together the economic,

Figure 8.1 In October 2003, these women in Kabul, Afghanistan are clad in traditional *burkas* from head to toe to go window shopping for the latest styles.

political, and cultural possibilities of Turkey's attempts in this way:

> As part of a slate of reforms aimed at securing membership in the European Union, Turkey's ruling party has proposed a major overhaul of the country's criminal code .... Prompted by a coalition of women's groups, it includes stronger laws against rape, sexual assault, and sexual harassment. Unfortunately, several other laws are regressive, seeking to codify in law beliefs and practices that reflect the party's own conservative Islamic roots rather than the European Union's modern vision of human rights.[67]

There is a less-obvious way in which women are involved in globalization's web. As Barbara Ehrenreich and Arlie Russell Hochschild put it in the introduction to their book of essays, *Global Woman: Nannies, Maids, and Sex Workers in the New Economy*, "Thanks to the process we loosely call 'globalization,' women are on the move as never before in history." The women who are most on the move, according to these authors, are an unprecedented flood of female immigrants to America and Europe who do work that had been done by wives and mothers in those homes:

> This is the female underside of globalization, whereby millions of [females] from poor countries in the south migrate to do the "women's work" of the north—work that affluent women are no longer able or willing to do. . . . While the European or American woman commutes to work an average of twenty-eight minutes a day, many nannies from the Philippines, Sri Lanka, and India cross the globe to get their jobs. Some female migrants from the Third World do find something like "liberation," or at least the chance to become independent breadwinners and to improve their children's material chances. Other, less fortunate migrant women end up in the control of criminal employers. . . . But even in more typical cases, where benign employers pay wages on time, Third World migrant women [overwhelmingly people of color] achieve their success only by assuming the cast-off domestic roles of middle- and high-income women in the First World.[68]

These women carry their cultures with them, and their languages and their habits of mind, even as global culture infiltrates the previously closed spheres of their home cultures. This is as apt a metaphor as any for understanding the many dynamic flows involved in globalization and of resisting the notion that globalization is only a "pull" towards a "global village."

Conclusions

Seen in the broadest possible terms, globalization is a phenomenon that has five essential components, all of which move at varying speeds throughout the world: finance, culture, media images, technology, and people. The primary focus of this volume has been on the dissemination of culture—the ideas that affect daily human existence.

Finance, which is extensively covered in other volumes in this series, refers to the movement of money across national boundaries as it seeks profit. This can include investment in roads, technologies, and so on in developing countries so that natural resources (raw materials) can be used in the manufacture of products destined for world markets. It can also include the movement of capital as it seeks to make money *on* money: currency values fluctuate relative to each other, and by "trading" money, it is possible to *make* money on these small currency-value differences. Thus, one can make money on the difference between the relative values of, for example, the American dollar and the Japanese yen.

This volume has linked together the last four items in the list. Ideas flow from cultural groups in a number of ways. The movement of people from place to place has obvious implications for the culture of a given geographic location because people are carriers of culture. The worldwide proliferation of media images via the Internet, television, and the like is a function of technological changes in communications. The computer revolution and the wide availability of cellular and other technologies have made the movement of ideas via media astonishingly fast in the vast majority of the world.

Ideologies, principles of thought that often emanate (via people and media) from the First World (the industrialized, developed world) are introduced into Third-World cultures (the undeveloped bulk of the world, such as much of Africa). These ideologies include elements that we have discussed under the general term of modernism (innovation, rationalism versus belief; urbanization versus agricultural existence; individualism versus collectivist thought). The more concrete consequences of modernism (which we can call "modernist culture" because this habit of mind has implications for action on the part of peoples around the world) include movements in favor of democratic self-determination, human rights, and environmental awareness.

The issue of culture in its globalizing form is a particularly contested one: echoes of colonialism (think of the justifications stated and implied in Kipling's "The White Man's Burden," for example) are embedded in the fear of cultural groups around the world that their unique diversity and integrity will be overwhelmed by a uniform mass culture attached to all the tentacles of global capital's quest for profit. There is a very strong backlash against globalization's modernizing face that requires careful attention.

For example, in India, national protections have been set up to protect the indigenous national film industry, termed "Bollywood", from extinction in the face of Hollywood's unstoppable market presence. Some countries such as North Korea control all communications in the country so that their national ideology is not eroded by the individual consumption of Western culture and its trailing ideologies.

The most powerful resistance to globalization's cultural influence, however, is actually a backlash against modernism itself: the rise of fundamentalist religious culture—and not just Islamic fundamentalism, but activist strains of evangelical Christianity and many other religions—as it challenges the scientific empiricism and rationality of Western modernism as a whole (Figure 9.1). That challenge affects all the subsets of the modernist ideology, including its most recent aspect: globalization. This challenge also often uses the very tools that modernism has created, choosing whatever techniques will serve the fundamentalist embrace of belief over inquiry. For example, a recent Internet search of the term "Islamic fundamentalism" uncovered 153,000 websites— many with multiple links of their own—that allow for the creation of virtual communities unlinked to location that use technology to challenge technology's rationalistic primacy.

As we have also noted, postmodernism's embrace of the fragment, of incoherence over coherence, and of parts rather than a whole, challenges modernism's certainty by insisting upon rational skepticism. One of the reasons that we treated the Sapir-Whorf theory of language and the concept of language as a filtering map individuals use to understand the world is rooted in the relativistic philosophy of language. Postmodernism assumes relativism. As one linguist puts it,

> Taken consistently, the Sapir-Whorf theory means that language is a subjective agreement by a group of people to conceptualize and verbalize their perceptions of reality in a certain way. The theory also means that the differences between languages are

Figure 9.1 The most powerful resistance to the cultural influence of globalization may be the rise of religious fundamentalism, such as that which resulted in deposing the Shah of Iran in 1979. This demonstration took place outside the U.S. Embassy in Tehran in 1979.

differences between conceptual interpretations of reality. The theory states that it upholds the "relativity of all conceptual systems," thereby excluding the possibility of an objective conceptual system. . . . The Sapir-Whorf theory is currently considered too extreme in scholarly circles.[69]

We have already observed that there is substantial disagreement among linguists over this essentially anthropological view of language.

Further, it is unwise to assume the inevitability of cultural trends such as the overwhelming dominance of English as a replacement for all other languages. In fact, a recent Associated Press report notes that some predict the opposite. British language expert David Graddol presented research that claimed that "the share of the world's population that speaks English as a native language is falling . . . . Monolingual speakers of any variety of English—English or British—will experience increasing difficulty in employment and political life, and are likely to become bewildered by many aspects of society and culture around them."[70] This same researcher projects that Hindi-Urdu speakers will outnumber English speakers by 2050.

Students are urged to consult other volumes in this series for treatment of the specifics of some of these issues. For example, the volume on globalization and labor relations treats the status of workers in far-flung parts of the globe as they manufacture (or service) products used in the First World. There are obvious implications (in financial terms, in cultural terms, and in ideological terms) for the role of labor-capital relationships insofar as they affect cultural change. Interested thinkers on this relationship will do what all thinkers do as a matter of course: they will synthesize disparate parts of a situation, creating a "synthetic" whole that is more than the sum of its parts. This has been the procedure followed in this volume.

The concepts of modernism and postmodernism have helped us to establish a foundation for understanding the movement toward cultural homogenization that is most shallowly understood as the "McDonaldization of the world." A more thoughtful approach puts it in this way:

Postmodernism is both a symptom and a powerful cultural image of the swing away from the conceptualization of global culture less in terms of alleged homogenizing processes (e.g., theories which present cultural imperialism, Americanization and mass consumer culture as a proto-universal culture riding on the back of Western economic and political domination) and more in terms of the diversity, variety, and richness of popular and local discourses, codes and practices which resist and play-back systemicity and order.[71]

By showing manifestations of the vast concept of globalization in its cultural moments, this volume has presented ideas that require some synthesis. *You* are part of globalization. If you become a better consumer of your own culture(s) by investigating specific examples of "culture"—whether it's a piece of clothing, a popular song, a "big idea," or an ideological assumption with which you are expected to automatically agree (without thought), you will become more than a passive carrier of others' ideologies. You will become a global thinker.

Culture—Those things that people do and say every day. Culture is the enactment of ideology.

Commodity culture—The belief that objects—commodities—are a necessary component of a life well lived. Its characteristics include the ready availability, and desirability, of material aspects of the cultures of the industrialized world.

Cultural critics—Those who study the various creations of the world without regard to the classic or elite appeal of such creations; they engage in what is generally referred to as cultural studies.

Cultural imperialism—The belief that one culture (often a national one) is imposing its ideas of appropriateness on another. This imposition is never simple and is never complete.

Cultural space—Public space that is marked by kinship, ethnic, or national cultural symbolic and vernacular interactions.

Economic liberalization—The loosening of national trade barriers, allowing capital and goods (and ideas, commodity culture, and, ultimately, modernism) to flow freely worldwide.

Elite—A small, powerful group at the top of a social pyramid.

Globalization—The general term for the integration and worldwide flow of financial (economic), cultural, political, technological, and ideological activities.

Ideology—The set of beliefs and principles that guide your everyday actions. These principles are often—but not always—unacknowledged by those who hold them.

Indigenous—Native people.

Lingua franca—A common language, a language of political power. In Europe until about 1700, the lingua franca was Latin.

Logical fallacy—An error in logical argument that is independent of the truth of the premises; it is a flaw in the structure of an argument, as opposed to an error in its premises.

Modernism—The set of ideological principles that underpin the modern nation–state system of political governance. These principles include an implied faith in the power of reason (evidenced in the primacy of science and technology over religious belief), the importance of the individual (and by extension of democratic principles and human rights), urbanization, and universal education.

Paradigm—A word that refers to the overall set of assumptions behind the way the world works.

Postmodernism—Skepticism about the optimistic faith in reason that exemplifies modernism. It is characterized by fragmentation, incoherence, and partial (relative) truths rather than grand, overarching explanations.

Symbol—An object, sound, or image that stands for or represents an idea, concept, or quality; a symbol is an example of a shared ideological bond.

Vernacular interaction—Normal, everyday social involvement with others.

Virtual community—Those who share culture at a distance, usually through technology.

Wage inequality—A measure of the relative distributions of incomes; this measure tracks the disparity within countries of high- and low-wage earners.

1 Quoted in Mike Featherstone, ed., *Global Culture: Nationalism, Globalization and Modernity*. London: Sage Publications, 1990, p. 295.

2 Quoted in Thomas Friedman, *The Lexus and the Olive Tree*. New York: Farrar, Straus and Giroux, 2000, p. 68.

3 Quoted in Joseph Stiglitz, *Globalization and Its Discontents*. New York: W. W. Norton, 2003, p. 4.

4 Quoted in David Morris, "Globalism," *Utne Reader* (Nov./Dec. 1988; reprinted March/April 1994), p. 73.

5 Quoted in Friedman, *The Lexus and the Olive Tree*, p. 7.

6 Ibid., p. 8.

7 Quoted in Sarah Anderson and John Cavanaugh, *Field Guide to the Global Economy*. New York: The New Press, 2000, p. 52.

8 Quoted in Albert Berry, Susan Horton, and Dipak Mazumdar, "Globalization, Adjustment, Inequality, and Poverty," *United Nations Human Development Papers 1997*, p. 22. Figures cited in Anderson and Cavanaugh, *Field Guide to the Global Economy*, p. 52.

9 Ibid.

10 Quoted in Tyler Cowen, "The Fate of Culture: Two Faces of Globalization," *The Wilson Quarterly* (Autumn 2002), p. 78.

11 Cited by Mourad Habachi of the English Institute of Casablanca, Morocco, "Globalization of Economy, The English Language and The Department of Economics in Morocco," 30th Annual Third World Conference, Chicago, Illinois, March 5, 2004.

12 Quoted in John Tomlinson, *Globalization and Culture*. Chicago: The University of Chicago Press, 1999, p. 20.

13 Quoted in Ross Murfin and Supryia M. Ray, eds., *The Bedford Glossary of Critical and Literary Terms*. Boston and New York: Bedford Books, 1997, p. 164.

14 An interesting review of this "split" can be found by comparing two texts: Dick Hebdige's classic, *Subculture: The Meaning of Style* (London: Methuen, 1979) and David Muggleton's edgy response to Hebdige entitled *Inside Subculture: The Postmodern Meaning of Style* (Oxford and New York: Berg, 2000).

15 Quoted in Murfin and Ray, *The Bedford Glossary of Critical and Literary Terms*, p. 164.

16 Ibid.

17 In an interview with the author (3 September 2004); Information available at *http://www.martinspencer.org*.

18 Quoted in Rob Walker, "Emily Says: How a Goth-girl face designed to promote a clothing line wound up with its own story line," *The New York Times Magazine* (August 15, 2004), p. 22.

19 Quoted on *http://www.matmice.com/home/emilythestrange13*.

20 Quoted in Walker, "*Emily Says*," p. 22.

21 Ibid.

22 Quoted in Arthur Lubow, "Cult Figures: How a Hong Kong Artist and his followers launched a global craze for . . . vinyl dolls?" *The New York Times Magazine* (August 15, 2004), p. 25.

23 Quoted in Tomlinson, *Globalization and Culture*, p. 20.

24 Quoted in Eric R. Wolf, *Europe and the People Without History*. Berkeley, CA: University of California Press 1997 [1982]), p. 71.

25 Ibid.

26 Quoted in Jaroslav Pelikan, *The Excellent Empire*. San Francisco: Harper & Row, 1987, p. 109.

27 Ibid.

28 Quoted in Denis Judd, *Empire: The British Imperial Experience from 1765 to the Present*. New York: Basic Books, 1996, p. 7.

29 Tyler Cowen, "The Fate of Culture: Two Faces of Globalization," *The Wilson Quarterly* (vol. 26.4): 78.

30 Quoted in "Berlin Conference of 1884-1885 to Divide Africa"; at *http://geography.com/cs/politicalgeog/a/berlinconferenc.htm.*

31 Cowen, "The Fate of Culture," p. 79.

32 See, for example, Cowen, "The Fate of Culture," p. 80.

33 Ward L. Kaiser and Denis Wood, *Seeing Through Maps: the Power of Images to Shape Our World View.* Amherst, Mass.: ODT, Inc., 2001.

34 Ibid., p. 4.

35 For more information, and a variety of other types of maps, including one which turns the world "upside-down," access the links at *http://www.seeingmaps.com.*

36 Quoted in *The Longman Anthology of World Literature Volume E: The Nineteenth Century,* Marshall Brown and Bruce Robbins, eds. New York: Pearson, 2004, p. 6.

37 Quoted in Gabriele Schwab, "Traveling literature, traveling theory: literature and cultural contact between East and West," *Studies in the Humanities* vol. 29.1 (June 2002): 5. Reprinted by permission.

38 Ibid.

39 Ibid.

40 Ibid., p. 6.

41 Quoted in Fredric Jameson, *The Prison-House of Language.* Princeton, N.J.: Princeton University Press, 1972, p. 1.

42 Quoted in Robin Dunbar, Chris Knight and Camilla Powers, eds., *The Evolution of Culture: An Inter-disciplinary View.* New Brunswick, N.J.: Rutgers University Press, 1999, p. 173.

43 Quoted in Michelle Fram-Cohen, "Reality, Language, Translation: What Makes Translation Possible." Paper presented at the American Translators Association Conference, Miami, 1985. Available at *http://enlightenment.supersaturated.com/essays/text/michelleframcohen/possibilityoftranslation.html.*

44 Quoted in Dunbar, et al., *The Evolution of Culture,* p. 221.

45 Ibid., p. 220.

46 Quoted in Sheldon Smith and Philip D. Young, *Cultural Anthropology: Understanding a World in Transition.* Boston and London: Allyn & Bacon, 1998, p. 48

47 Quoted in Steven Pinker, *The Language Instinct.* New York: William Morrow, 1994, pp. 17–18.

48 Ibid., p. 64.

49 Quoted on the website of Congressman Robert Dornan: *http://www.bobdornan.com/english.html.*

50 Quoted on the website of the Horatio Alger Society, *http://www.ihot.com/~has.*

51 Quoted on the website of the Horatio Alger Association for Distinguished Americans, *http://www.horatioalger.com.*

52 Quoted in Michael Valdez Moses, *The Novel and the Globalization of Culture.* New York and Oxford: Oxford University Press, 1995, p.6.

53 Quoted in Thomas Friedman, *The Lexus and the Olive Tree.* New York: Farrar, Straus and Giroux, p. 7.

54 Ibid., p. 8.

55 Quoted in "Did David Hasselhoff really help end the Cold War?" The BBC News' World Edition online (February 6, 2004). Available online at *http://news.bbc.co.uk/1/hi/magazine/3465301.stm.*

56 Ibid.

57 Frank Kessler, Catriona Nally, and Luke Cairney, "The Millenium Challenge Account: Bush Administration Initiatives in Development Assistance," presented at the 30th Annual Third World

Conference, Chicago, Illinois, March 4, 2004; Paolo Paiscolon, "The Millenium Challenge Account: Creating Effective Development Assistance," in *Agenda 2003, www.heritage.org/agenda.*

58 Kessler et al., "The Millenium Challenge Account

59 Quoted in *The Guardian Unlimited* online (February 25, 2004). Available at *http://www.guardian.co.uk/ g2/story/0,3604,1155254,00.html.*

60 Ibid.

61 Ibid.

62 Ibid.

63 Ibid.

64 Ibid.

65 Ibid.

66 Ibid.

67 Quoted in The *New York Times* online (September 12, 2004): *http://www.nytimes.com/2004/09/12/ opinion/12sun3.html.*

68 Quoted in Barbara Ehrenreich and Arlie Russell Hochschild, eds., *Global Woman: Nannies, Maids, and Sex Workers in the New Economy.* New York: Metropolitan Books, 2002, p. 3.

69 Quoted in Fram-Cohen, "Reality, Language, Translation."

70 Quoted in "English dropping in dominance, researcher says," Associated Press wire story reprinted in *The Daily Star*, Oneonta, N.Y. (February, 28, 2004), p. A7.

71 Quoted in Mike Featherstone, ed., *Global Culture: Nationalism, Globalization and Modernity.* London: Sage Publications, 1990, p. 2.

Anderson, Sarah, and John Cavanaugh. *Field Guide to the Global Economy.* New York: The New Press, 2000.

Barbieri, Katherine. *The Liberal Illusion: Does Trade Promote Peace?* Ann Arbor, MI: The University of Michigan Press, 2002.

Brown, Marshall, and Bruce Robbins, eds. *The Longman Anthology of World Literature Volume E: The Nineteenth Century.* New York: Pearson, 2004.

Chappell, Warren. *A Short History of the Printed Word.* Boston: Nonpareil Books, 1970.

Cowen, Tyler. "The Fate of Culture: the Two Faces of Globalization," *The Wilson Quarterly* 26, no.1 (Autumn 2002): 78-85.

Dunbar, Robin, Chris Knight, and Camilla Power, eds. *The Evolution of Culture: An Interdisciplinary View.* New Brunswick, N.J.: Rutgers University Press, 1999.

Eisenstein, Elizabeth. *The Printing Press as an Agent of Change: Communications and Transformations in Early-modern Europe* (Volume I). Cambridge and London: Cambridge University Press, 1979.

Ehrenreich, Barbara, and Arlie Russell Hochschild. *Global Woman: Nannies, Maids, and Sex Workers in the New Economy.* New York: Metropolitan Books, 2002.

Featherstone, Mike, ed. *Global Culture: Nationalism, Globalization and Modernity.* London: Sage Publications, 1990.

Fram-Cohen, Michelle. "Reality, Language, Translation: What makes Translation Possible." Paper presented at the American Translators Association Conference, Miami, 1985. Available at *http://enlightenment.supersaturated.com/essays/text/michelleframcohen/ possibilityoftranslation.html.*

Friedman, Thomas L. *The Lexus and The Olive Tree,* New York: Farrar, Straus and Giroux, 1999.

Graham, Gerald S. *A Concise History of the British Empire.* London: Thames and Hudson, Ltd., 1978.

Hebdige, Dick. *Subculture: The Meaning of Style.* London: Methuen, 1979.

Holtgraves, Thomas M. *Language as Social Action: Social Psychology and Language Use.* Mahwah, NJ: Lawrence Erlbaum Associates, 2002.

James, Harold. *The End of Globalization: Lessons from the Great Depression.* Cambridge, MA: Harvard University Press, 2001.

Jameson, Fredric. *The Prison-House of Language.* Princeton, NJ: Princeton University Press, 1972.

Judd, Denis. *Empire: The British Imperial Experience, from 1765 to the Present.* London and New York: Basic Books, 1996.

Kagan, Donald, ed. *Decline and Fall of the Roman Empire: Why Did It Collapse?* Boston: D.C. Heath and Co., 1962.

Kaiser, Ward L., and Denis Wood. *Seeing Through Maps: The Power of Images to Shape Our World View.* Amherst, MA: ODT, Inc., 2001.

Katz, Solomon. *The Decline of Rome and the Rise of Mediaeval Europe.* Ithaca, NY: Cornell University Press, 1963.

Kuhl, Jackson. "Tempest in a Teapot: Starbucks Invades the World," *Reason* 34 (January 2003): 55–56.

Lubow, Arthur. "Cult Figures: How a Hong Kong Artist and His Followers Launched a Global Craze for . . . Vinyl Dolls?" The *New York Times Magazine* (August 15, 2004): 25.

Morris, David. "Globalism," *Utne Reader* (Nov./Dec. 1988; reprinted March/April 1994): 73.

Moses, Michael Valdez. *The Novel and the Globalization of Culture.* Oxford and New York: The Oxford University Press, 1995.

Muggleton, David. *Inside Subculture: The Postmodern Meaning of Style.* Oxford and New York: Berg, 2000.

Murfin, Ross, and Supryia M. Ray, eds. *The Bedford Glossary of Critical and Literary Terms.* Boston and New York: Bedford Books, 1997.

Pelikan, Jaroslav. *The Excellent Empire: The Fall of Rome and the Triumph of the Church.* San Francisco: Harper & Row, 1987.

Pinker, Steven. *The Language Instinct.* New York: William Morrow and Company, Inc., 1994.

Schwab, Gabriele. "Traveling Literature, Traveling Theory: Literature and Cultural Contact between East and West." *Studies in the Humanities* 26, no. 1 (June 2002): 5–14.

Smith, Sheldon and Philip D. Young. *Cultural Anthropology: Understanding a World in Transition.* Boston and London: Allyn and Bacon, 1998.

Stiglitz, Joseph E. *Globalization and Its Discontents.* New York: W.W. Norton, 2002.

Tomlinson, John. *Globalization and Culture.* Chicago: The University of Chicago Press, 1999.

Walker, Rob. "Emily Says: How a Goth-Girl Face Designed to Promote a Clothing Line Wound Up with Its Own Story Line." The *New York Times Magazine* (August 15, 2004): 22.

Wolf, Eric R. *Europe and the People Without History.* Berkeley, CA: University of California Press, 1997 [1982].

Anderson, Sarah, and John Cavanaugh. *Field Guide to the Global Economy.* New York: The New Press, 2000.

Friedman, Thomas L. *The Lexus and The Olive Tree.* New York: Farrar, Straus and Giroux, 1999.

Hebdige, Dick. *Subculture: The Meaning of Style.* London: Methuen, 1979.

Kaiser, Ward L., and Denis Wood. *Seeing Through Maps: The Power of Images to Shape Our World View.* Amherst, MA: ODT, Inc., 2001.

Muggleton, David. *Inside Subculture: The Postmodern Meaning of Style.* Oxford and New York: Berg, 2000.

Pinker, Steven. *The Language Instinct.* New York: William Morrow, 1994.

Tomlinson, John. *Globalization and Culture.* Chicago: The University of Chicago Press, 1999.

PICTURE CREDITS

page:

16: Associated Press, AP
18: © Vittoriano Rastelli/CORBIS
33: © Bettmann/CORBIS
36: Courtesy of www.EmilyStrange.com
39: Associated Press, AP/Francois Mori
40: All Rights Reserved, courtesy of Crazysmiles Co./Michael Lau
44: Library of Congress
48: © Peter Lamb
53: © Peter Lamb
58: Reproduced from SEEING THROUGH MAPS by Kaiser and Wood, 2001, ODT, Inc., Amherst, MA. Originally appeared in *Map Projections-A Working Manual*, John P. Snyder, USGS Professional Paper 1935, 1987, Washington D.C. (page 40).
59: Reproduced from SEEING THROUGH MAPS by Kaiser and Wood, 2001, ODT, Inc., Amherst, MA. Originally drawn by Roy Collins in Wellman Chamberlin's *The Round Earth on Flat Paper*, National Geographic Society, 1947, 1950. Washington D.C. (pages 80-81).
61: © Peter Lamb
62: The Peters Projection World Map was produced with the support of the United Nations Development Programme. For maps and other related teaching materials contact: ODT, Inc., PO Box 134, Amherst MA 01004 USA; (800-736-1293; Fax: 413-549-3503; E-mail: odt-store@odt.org).
70: © Peter Lamb
83: Associated Press, AP/Jeff Widener
89: Associated Press, AP/
94: Associated Press, AP/Eckehard Schulz
104: Associated Press, AP/Stephen Thorne
109: Associated Press, AP

Cover: © James Marshall/CORBIS

Richard Lee received his Ph.D. in comparative literature from Rutgers University, where he studied European and African literatures. He is currently an assistant professor of English at the State University of New York's College at Oneonta. He received a SUNY Chancellor's Award for Excellence in Teaching in 2004; he is also the recipient of other awards for teaching and mentoring undergraduates. Dr. Lee is the Director of the Cooper Seminar— a scholarly conference held biennially for the past thirty years in upstate New York, which focuses on the texts and contexts of James Fenimore Cooper and related nineteenth-century American authors. Recent publications include essays on cross-cultural pedagogy, postmodernism, numerous encyclopedia articles on British and African writers, and several monographs on contemporary American short-story writers. He co-edited *The Dictionary of Literary Biography: American Short-Story Writers since WWII (third series)*; he is currently compiling another volume for this series.

James Bacchus is Chairman of the Global Trade Practice Group of the international law firm Greenberg Traurig, Professional Association. He is also a visiting professor of international law at Vanderbilt University Law School. He served previously as a special assistant to the United States Trade Representative; as a Member of the Congress of the United States, from Florida; and as a Member, for eight years, and Chairman, for two terms, of the Appellate Body of the World Trade Organization. His book, *Trade and Freedom*, was published by Cameron May in London in 2004, and is now in its third edition worldwide.

Ilan Alon, Ph.D, is Associate Professor of International Business at the Crummer Graduate School of Business of Rollins College. He holds a Ph.D in International Business and Economics from Kent State University. He currently teaches courses on Business in the Global Environment and Emerging Markets: China in the business curriculum as well as International Trade and Economics in the economics curriculum.